The Grief Care Kit

Bereavement Resources for Counselors and Recovery Group Leaders

Harold Ivan Smith

BEACON HILL PRESS
OF KANSAS CITY

First edition 2002
Second edition 2008, with title change

ISBN: 978-0-8341-2382-3

Printed in the
United States of America

Cover Design by Arthur Cherry
Interior Design by Sharon Page

Library of Congress Cataloging-in-Publication Data

Smith, Harold Ivan, 1947-
The grief care kit : bereavement resources for counselors and recovery group leaders / Harold Ivan Smith.
p. cm.— (LifeStream resources)
Includes bibliographical references.
ISBN 978-0-8341-2382-3 (pbk., with accompanying cd and dvd resources)
1. Church work with the bereaved. 2. Grief. I. Title.

BV4330 .S575 2008
259'.6—dc22

2008014271

10 9 8 7 6 5 4 3

CONTENTS

INTRODUCTION

BENEFITS OF THIS RESOURCE

Tragedy strikes everyone. Some tragedies affect lots of people. Other tragedies affect one family at a time. Whatever the nature of the loss, this resource will help pastors, lay leaders, and grief support group leaders make a difference in caring for grievers in their congregations and their communities.

This resource will help you do the following:

- Develop and implement a healthy philosophy of grief care in the local church.
- Communicate with the families and individuals touched by the loss. Thirty sample letters will help pastors and care leaders write meaningful letters of comfort.
- Design more meaningful funeral and memorial services.
- Create a mutual-help group for grieving persons.
- Acknowledge and support grieving children.
- Respond to adolescents in grief.
- Provide resources for grievers on Mother's Day and the Christmas holidays.

THE GRIEF CARE KIT DVD AND CD

This kit includes a video workshop, "Ministering in Times of Loss," on DVD. The workshop features the author instructing a group of participants in the practice of grief ministry. A fill-in-the-blank handout designed to accompany the video is included on the kit's CD for printing and duplication.

Also on the CD are text files of letters, naming rituals, hymns, and other resources found in this booklet. These documents are printable and in some cases adaptable for the preparation of handouts, insertion in letters, and other uses. In addition, the CD contains audio files of the hymns "Day by Day," "Precious Memories," "Does Jesus Care?" "What a Friend We Have in Jesus," "He Keeps Me Singing," "It Is Well with My Soul," and "He Giveth More Grace."

Because the CD has been designed to operate initially as a music CD, it may trigger the music auto-play feature on your computer. If this happens when you desire to access the text files, you will need to close the corresponding pop-up media player and open the CD using Microsoft Windows Explorer. You will then be able access and open the documents as needed. For further information, see the readme file contained on the CD.

1

ASSISTING THE GRIEVING IN A "GRIEF-LITE" CULTURE

▶ Pastor David Verzyl served heroically as a chaplain at the Morgue Unit at Ground Zero following the September 11 disaster. Months after many people had "moved on," Pastor Verzyl was still on the scene making a difference in the lives of workers at Ground Zero and in the lives of his own congregation, the Kingston Church of the Nazarene. Ministry takes place, unfortunately, in a society that is impatient with mourning. But Pastor Verzyl could never have made an impact had he believed he was to "hurry along" grievers. He gave the grievers with whom he came in close contact generous chunks of time; he built bridges into their grief.

The enormity of David's work is overwhelming—especially in this "grief-lite" culture we live in. "Get over it." "Go on with your life." For the sensitive pastor, grief ministry is more than platitudes and pats on the back. It's a meaningful opportunity to share the person of Christ with the walking wounded among us.

There's a lot of grief theory pastors use. Perhaps the most widely used, but no longer endorsed by grief educators and therapists, is Elisabeth Kübler-Ross's "five stages" and its many variations. Admittedly, Dr. Kübler-Ross got people more comfortable talking about grief with her descriptions of the stages: denial, anger, bargaining, acceptance, and growth. However, these stages are too limiting and too passive to capture the grief experience of most individuals.

When Moses came down from the mountain with the Ten Commandments, some ministers, counselors, and facilitators presume he had the "five stages of grief" tucked under the other arm. Whatever the loss, these caregivers dish out a generous helping of the stages of grief—anger, denial, bargaining, acceptance, and growth. Like elixirs once sold at county fairs, these stages are touted as being good for whatever grief ails you.

Yet the grief-stages concept is only a theory. Look at the inside of your right thumb. Six and a half billion people occupy planet Earth. No one has a thumbprint like yours. God went to a lot of trouble to make your thumbprint unique. Your "griefprint" is unique too. No two people grieve exactly the same way.

Victoria Alexander has identified three needs of individuals grappling with loss.[1]

1. Grievers need to find words for the loss. Many times people who grieve are at a loss for words, especially early in the grief experience. They say they were flabbergasted, speechless, or numb. Some will never forget those first "O God, no!" moments when death invaded their lives. Many will never forget their first faltering attempts to respond to the question, "What happened?" or "How are you holding up?" Nor will some ever forget the wounds inflicted by worn clichés and insensitivity.

John Dasburg, CEO of Burger King, lost his six-year-old daughter in 1988 as a result of a school-van accident. When others ask him "When will the pain go away?" Dasburg stuns many with his answer, "Never."

"No one can stand it, the pain is so intense. It has never gone away from me. You learn to live with it, you get accustomed to it, you accommodate it."[2]

Unfortunately, in our quick-fix culture, too many expect grievers to move on and get over it. We live in a "grief-lite" culture.

If you love someone and you "lose" him or her—you will grieve. The question is, Can you grieve openly? Can you talk about the grief? How can you acknowledge loss until you try out words?

One of the greatest gifts ministers, counselors, and facilitators can offer is patience as someone sorts words. Some individuals struggle. They don't know how to say what they are thinking. In the grief groups I lead, I ask, "Have you ever played Scrabble? You shake the lettered tiles in a little container, then spill them out. You sort through the letters and make up a word." Grief is a shaking experience that thoroughly scrambles our thoughts, feelings, and beliefs.

Following a death, one of the kindest things a pastor can do is to string together a coherent sentence, then, perhaps, a paragraph. Narratives get constructed a word at a time.

2. Grievers need to say the words aloud. You've heard, "What good is talking about it going to do?" The answer is, "A lot." Some people experience a word logjam. One of the great gifts of a sovereign God is support groups and counselors. In the not too distant past, grievers got through a loss the best way they could. What would some lives be like if the bereaving could have found a caring mutual-help group where they could have talked out the devastation they had experienced and have learned from the experiences of others?

3. Grievers need to know that the words have been heard. Remember the question, "If a tree falls in the forest and no one hears it—was there any sound?" If a person is grieving and no one hears—or "receives" that grief—is it really grief? God invented tears. When tears run down our face, we need someone who notices and asks, "What's wrong?" Grievers' laments contain words that can be raw and caustic. Paraphrasing the prophet Jeremiah's experience, words are "in my heart like a fire, a fire shut up in my bones. I am weary of holding it in; indeed, I cannot" (Jer. 20:9).

The power of words is illustrated in Jesus' caring for Martha and Mary following the death of their brother, Lazarus. "If you had been here, my brother would not have died" (John 11:21, 32), the sisters exclaimed as they confronted Jesus. The words stung Jesus, who was grieving (v. 33).

Sometimes words erupt. Sometimes they won't come. Sometimes it takes years.

Four hundred and fifty years ago a caring minister penned an invitation that is pertinent today: "Then let him come to me . . . or some other discreet and learned minister of God's word and open his grief that he may receive counsel, and advice, and comfort" (*Book of Common Prayer* [1552]).

Grief sharers are called to "receive the narratives" of the broken, lost, confused, bewildered, and wounded.[3] Too often, in these days of time-framed ministry, with more demands than a human can meet, pastors serve like physicians who allot seven minutes to "see" a patient. One remarkable moment in the New Testament is when Jesus chided Simon the Pharisee, "Do you see this woman?" (Luke 7:44). I think he actually asked, "Do you see *this* woman?" Jesus might ask you as a pastor or facilitator, "Do you see *this* griever?" You may have heard lots of loss stories—but you have not heard *this* individual's lament.

To this griever or family it will not matter how "good" you were with previous grievers. How available are you in *this* loss?

As you listen to a griever's description of loss, consider the possibility that underneath the rubble of this loss—or this latest sorrow—is a smoldering unhealed, unfinished loss. Remember the fires that burned for months in the ruins of the World Trade Center rubble? All it took was a little wind to stir the embers into a fire. Many grievers have accumulated thick layers of ash and tons of emotional rubble over their souls. Jesus invites us to lead the bereaving toward a clearing away of the layers of wounds.

THE TASKS OF GRIEF

J. William Worden, the leading American authority on grief therapy, identifies four "tasks" or "to dos" for grievers. His proactive approach contrasts with the more passive "get through it the best way you can" stages of grief. This approach may be useful for some persons you counsel.

One of the wildest adventures of my life was rafting a portion of the Chattooga River in South Carolina (the river Burt Reynolds made famous in the movie *Deliverance*). Some persons step into rafts and let the river take charge. It's no surprise that a few of these drown! On its own the Chattooga will take rafters over perilous rapids (rather than through them or along the bank) where enormous tree branches can do serious damage to the head. Wise adventurers rely on a navigator to guide them down the dangerous course of this powerful river. It's the same river but a different experience.

Worden identifies these tasks to help grievers navigate their loss:

1. Accept the reality of the loss.
2. Work through to the pain of the loss.
3. Adjust to environments in which the person is missing.

4. Relocate emotionally, and memorialize the loved one.[4]

For people used to Day-Timers and PalmPilots or old-fashioned to-do lists scribbled on the back of envelopes, this task-oriented approach makes more sense than the more passive approach that just lets grief happen. It gives a sense of empowerment and some degree of control. Consider Worden's task list:

1. To accept the reality of the loss

Accepting that this loss has happened can be draining emotional and spiritual work. For example, many people are reluctant to acknowledge the finality of death.

Leaving a bedroom or office intact, some cling to the fantasy of the deceased coming back. A few construct elaborate alternative expectations to deny the painful reality. After her mother's death, one 10-year-old told friends that her mother had gotten tired of raising five children and had gone to live in California but someday would come back, and all would be well. Some grievers, who spent long hours and shouldered great responsibility as caregivers, find it difficult to reorganize their lives following the death of a loved one. To fully recognize a loss requires acknowledging that the loss is permanent. Sometimes a pastor or counselor must help grievers confront the pain created by the realities.

2. To work through to the pain of the loss

As we've mentioned, we live in a "grief-lite" culture. We pop pills to dodge or diffuse pain. What happens when you get a headache? Rather than asking "What is causing this?" you reach for an aspirin (or something stronger). Unfortunately, some misquote Worden, "To work through the pain of the loss." They skip the "to" before "the pain."

An old southern gospel song offers an insight: "No way around it, no way over it, no way under it." We go or grow through this loss. It's our decision.

3. To adjust to environments in which the person is missing

"I'll be seeing you in all the old familiar places . . ." We can't forget that place is an essential element in our memories. One widower described his difficulty attending worship services. "My wife sang in the choir for years, always on the front row. When the choir came in, she would always look for me, then smile. Every Sunday when the service starts and the choir comes in, I miss her smile. . . . some Sundays, I go late to avoid the memories."

4. To relocate emotionally and memorialize the loved one

Where is the person I have loved?

A griever with a confident concept of heaven can find comfort in the blessed hope of reunion, someday. This is undergirded with the clear testimony to faith in Jesus Christ as Lord and Savior. Some, however, do not have this confidence because of circumstances in the deceased's life.

Many grievers find it troublesome to "move on." Many feel powerless to accept the secondary losses (see page 13). Sometimes funeral directors find it necessary to say to a widow at her husband's grave, or parents at a child's grave, "It's time to leave the cemetery." A widow or widower or a parent cannot stay in the cemetery. How many have stayed behind in "emotional" cemeteries, deep in the crevices of the heart?

For me, one of the most moving passages in the Old Testament is the Genesis account of the death of Sarah: "Abraham went to mourn for Sarah and to weep over her" (Gen. 23:2). What was it like for Abraham those first nights after having slept with Sarah for more than a century? Yet Abraham did not pitch a tent over Sarah's grave. Rather, the Scriptures report, "And Abraham *stood up*" (v. 3, KJV, emphasis added).

After years of working with grieving persons, I am convinced that no one "gets over it." This loss is a permanent fixture in the typography of the landscape of the soul. Over time, with the support of people in a community of faith, individuals can rise up and with God's help integrate the loss into their life narratives. The loss becomes one theme but not the dominant theme in their life story. They are no longer paralyzed by the loss.

Some pastors and leaders use the word "recover" when talking about grief. This is ill advised because in too many minds "recovery" = "get over." Grievers will never "get over" their loss. They can, in time, with God's gracious, compassionate kindness—and the help of family, friends, and neighbors—integrate that loss into the "batter" of life. As a child I loved to watch my mother bake cakes (I got to lick the bowl). One thing that fascinated me was when she made red velvet cake on Saturdays. My mother often handed me the small bottle of red dye and said, "Shake in a few drops." After I did, my mother thoroughly "beat" those tiny drops into the batter until the batter became "red velvet."

Healthy grievers blend a loss into the batter of their lives, and they find ways to continue to cherish the memory of their loved one.

ADVICE FOR LEADER CARE FOR THE GRIEVING

1. Be a companion. Grieving persons need companions for the path and trail guides.[5] I have a friend who is taking off work for six months to hike the Appalachian Trail. He is reading every account and talking to as many Appalachians as possible. I am trying to be supportive by clipping articles I read about the trail. However, there is a one difference—I do not have Appalachian Trail dirt or mud on my boots. I have not "been there, done that." I like the Spanish word *compañero* or *acompaña*—"one who accompanies." The effectiveness of grief sharing is rarely the teaching but rather the supportive interaction of the path sharers.

2. Acknowledge the secondary losses. Secondary losses include the loss of a sexual partner, a second income, the one who knew how to "fix" the leaking faucet, the one who encouraged, the one who kept up the social connections with other persons, and so on. Coming home to an empty house, cooking for one, eating alone, and praying alone are secondary losses that can be spiritually troubling.

3. Help the griever refocus the horizon. "How can I live without him or her for the rest of my life?" "The rest of my life" can be a significant portion of time. Help the griever focus on one day's portion of the horizon. The future comes one day at a time (sometimes in one hour segments).

4. Listen all the way to the end of the griever's sentences. Although you are busy and this narrative sounds like ones you've heard before, give this griever your attention. It's tempting to assume you know where the sentences are going. Jesus' experience with the woman at the well is significant insight into Jesus' interruptibility. John reports, "Just then his disciples returned and were surprised to find him talking with a woman" (John 4:27). Jesus was not simply talking but also listening. Because Jesus listened, it became a life-changing moment, not only for the woman but for the villagers as well.

5. Warn about numbing behaviors. Many grievers want something to numb or diffuse the pain. Many pastors and facilitators are alert to the dangers of alcohol or drugs. But what about the person who dodges his or her pain by overworking or overeating? An addictive behavior can be anything that helps us escape the pain. It's no surprise that sex or pornography is increasingly used to take the edge off grief discomforts.

6. Ask, "Who is offering you advice?" Grievers may be overwhelmed sorting through conflicting advice. Some grievers feel an obligation to accept advice. That's why there is wisdom in urging grievers not to make any major decisions for a year.

7. Pray for/pray with this griever. Don't just use the cliché, "I will pray for you." Ask, "How can I pray for you?" Pray for the griever now in his or her presence.

8. Know resources for referral. Remember that for some widows or widowers, joint bank accounts can be frozen, credit cards discontinued, and so on. Remember that the cost of counseling care may be prohibitive. Where in your community of faith or your social community can an individual find help through your referral?

9. Take seriously any threat to harm anyone. You may want to make a covenant with the individual: While you are counseling with me or in this mutual-care grief group, you will not do anything violent to anyone—including yourself.

10. Anoint. James says, "Is any one of you in trouble? He should pray. . . . Is any one of you sick? He should call the elders of the church to pray over him and anoint him with oil in the name of the Lord" (James 5:13-14). While grief is not an illness, it can trigger illness. The Early Church did not have our sophisticated medical system, but it was never stingy with anointing oil.

11. Believe in a future for this individual. In the Old Testament, the man who rescued the prophet Jeremiah from sure death in a cistern was concerned about his own future. "The word of the LORD came to [Jeremiah]: 'Go and tell Ebed-Melech the Cushite'" that despite the chaos that would be the fate of Jerusalem at the hand of the Babylonians, "I will rescue you on that day . . . ; you will not be handed over to those you fear. I will save you" (Jer. 39:16-18). In the early days of loss, many grievers are overwhelmed by fears.

Your experience as a trail scout with others will put you in a place to companion this individual. You are in the unique position to take a sliver of hope in the future and place it in the palm of the hand of this griever. As pastor, counselor, or group facilitator you may have to squeeze the fingers of the griever around that sliver. The God who rescued a eunuch four millennia ago will rescue this individual. The words of Jeremiah come to mind, "'For I know the plans I have for you,' declares the LORD, 'plans to prosper you and not to harm you, plans to give you hope and a future'" (29:11).

Consider Linda's story. Life dumped on Linda. Her son died with AIDS. Her husband left her. Because she had been absent so much from work to care for her son, Linda lost her job. Because she lost her job, she soon lost her home. Those around Linda marveled, as she seemed to maintain a positive attitude and outlook on life.

"How can you manage to be so positive?" Linda's pastor asked.

"O pastor, every morning I vote."

"What?"

"Every morning when I wake up, I take a vote. 'All in favor of getting out of bed say, "Aye." Those opposed, "Nay." The motion carries. Get out of bed!' Then in the bathroom I take a second vote. 'All in favor of this being a good day say, "Aye." Those opposed, "Nay." The motion carries again. This will be a good day.'"

Linda could have pulled the covers over her head and lamented the unfairness of life. Rather, by partnering with God, she lived with her loses.

The great promise was seen by Isaiah: "The LORD will guide you always; he will satisfy your needs in a sun-scorched land and will strengthen your frame" (Isa. 58:11).

Sometimes a pastor, counselor, or facilitator must initially believe that promise for the griever.

Let God use you to make a difference in a griever's life.

NOTES

1. Victoria Alexander, *Words I Never Thought to Speak: Stories of Life in the Wake of Suicide* (New York: Lexington Books, 1991), 9.

2. Del Jones, "Burger King CEO Hopes to Help by Sharing His Grief," *USA Today,* 14 November 2001, 1B.

3. Richard Rohr, *Everything Belongs: The Gift of Contemplative Prayer* (New York: Crossroad, 2000), 111.

4. William J. Worden, *Grief Counseling and Grief Therapy: A Handbook for the Mental Health Practitioner,* 3d ed. (New York: Springer, 2002), 47.

5. Alan D. Wolfelt, "Companioning Versus Treating: Beyond the Medical Model of Bereavement Caregiving: Part 3," *The Forum* 24, no. 6 (November/December 1998): 3, 15.

A. Essentials for Grievers

The following touch points are designed as an overview of concepts that will help pastors build bridges with the bereaving. Most of these things you already know, but it may be a helpful resource for reviewing.

Pastors may also find these touch points helpful in doing "grief education" in a local congregation. Sometimes conflicts arise because members of a congregation do not understand a pastor's philosophy on grief care. The touch points might provide a wonderful resource for a prolonged conversation with a church board about how grief is shared in a local church. To be honest it may take time for a group of laity to "warm up" to the topic, but such a discussion could be valuable to the life of a congregation that, sooner or later, will be touched by grief.

Periodically, a pastor should spend some time reviewing these touch points and auditing his or her own servant care. What is it that I do well? What are some areas in which I could be more effective and more compassionate? These days there are lots of demands on a pastor's time, but few are more important than "being present" to the bereaving.

A pastor should, from time to time, preach about the ministry of grief sharing. Some of these touch points would be helpful in developing such a message, whether in a sermon format or perhaps a teaching format in a prayer meeting or workshop.

These touch points could be used to guide discussions as new staff members join the staff of a church, especially those with little previous exposure to dying, death, and bereavement.

Three essential things to remember

- Find words for the loss.
- Say the words aloud.
- Know that the words have been heard.

—Victoria Alexander[1]

"As we have opportunity, let us do good to all people, especially to those who belong to the family of believers" (Gal. 6:10).

"Grieving is a journey that teaches us how to love in a new way now that our loved one is no longer with us.

"Consciously remembering those who have died is the key that opens our hearts, that allows us to love them in new ways."

—Thomas Attig[2]

Steps toward grief resolution

- Helping the bereaved to admit that the loss has taken place and is final
- Helping the bereaved to experience and express all range of emotions, deep feelings, and private thoughts, including the pleasant and the unpleasant ones, as related to loss
- Helping the bereaved to release the lost object or deceased person by letting go, setting free, and saying good-bye
- Helping the bereaved to reinvest the mental and emotional energy consumed earlier in unsuccessful resolution of grief in new relationships, endeavors, people, and projects

—Naji Abi-Hashem[3]

The goal of grief counseling

To help the bereaved

- accommodate the loss
- complete the mourning process
- receive adequate nurture and support
- make necessary adjustments
- return to a certain degree of normal functioning

"The goal is to help the bereaved transform, reshape, reframe, and reinterpret the former relationship by giving loss a new value, place, and meaning.

"The purpose of grief counseling is not to bring the bereaved to a *griefless* state. That is not actually possible.

"Grieflessness is not a human condition.

"It is essential to allow the bereaved to move through the mourning process at their own pace and in their own style."

—Naji Abi-Hashem[4]

Four roles of grief for a congregation

- To accept the reality of the loss
- To give expression to the pain of the separation
- To begin to build a cherishable memory
- To experience the support of a community of persons gathered together to affirm the worth of the deceased and to assure the bereaved of available support

—Denman Dewey[5]

Obstacles that block grief resolution

- Persistent longing for the lost object/person
- Overidentification with the deceased
- Inability to cry or rage at the loss
- Misdirected anger or ambivalence toward the deceased
- Interlocking grief reactions due to previous losses
- Covert contacts with the deceased
- Unrevealed secrets and unfinished business
- Lack of social support
- Reinforcement from others to remain grief stricken

—F. T. Melges and D. DeMaso[6]

Factors in complicated mourning

- Recognize the loss.
  Acknowledge the death.
  Understand the death.
- React to the separation.
  Experience the pain.
  Feel, identify, accept, and give some form of expression to all the psychological reactions to the loss.
- Recollect and reexperience the deceased and the relationship.
  Review and remember realistically.
  Revive and reexperience the feelings.
- Relinquish the old attachments to the deceased and the old assumptive world.

- Readjust to move adaptively into the new world without forgetting the old.
  - Revise the old assumptive world.
  - Develop a new relationship with the deceased.
  - Adopt new ways of being in the world.
  - Form a new identity.
- Reinvest.

—Therese A. Rando[7]

Four primary tasks for bereaving

- To satisfy bodily needs and minimize physical distress in ways that are consistent with other values
- To maximize psychological security, autonomy, and richness in living
- To sustain and enhance those interpersonal attachments significant to the person concerned and to address the social implications of bereaving
- To identify, develop, or reaffirm social sources of spiritual energy and in so doing to foster hope

—adapted from Charles A. Corr[8]

NOTES

1. Victoria Alexander, *Words I Never Thought to Speak: Stories of Life in the Wake of Suicide* (New York: Lexington Books, 1991), 9.

2. Thomas Attig, *The Heart of Grief: Death and Search for Lasting Love* (New York: Oxford University Press, 2000), 27.

3. Naji Abi-Hashem, "Grief, Loss, and Bereavement: An Overview," *Journal of Psychology and Christianity* 18, no. 4 (1999): 321.

4. Ibid.

5. Denman Dewey, "When a Congregation Cares: Organizing Ministry to the Bereaved," *Death Studies* 12 (1988): 123-35.

6. F. T. Melges and D. DeMaso, "Grief-resolution Therapy: Re-living, Revising, and Revisiting," *American Journal of Psychotherapy* 34 (1980): 51-61.

7. Therese A. Rando, "The Increasing Prevalence of Complicated Mourning: The Onslaught Is Just Beginning," *Omega* 26 (1992-93): 45.

8. Charles A. Corr, "A Task-based Approach to Coping with Dying," in *The Path Ahead,* ed. Lynne Ann DeSpelder and Albert Lee Strickland (Mountain View, Calif.: Mayfield Publishing, 1995), 306.

B. Essentials for Grief Ministry to Children

Pastors and families face special challenges when helping young persons work through grief. Following are some tips and insights for guiding children and adolescents in the grieving process.

WHEN IT COMES TO GRIEF, CHILDREN SHOULD BE SEEN AND HEARD

"Children of all ages, alert to the world around them, know much more than we realize about death and dying. They respond to and understand their knowledge in unique ways." —Phyllis Silverman[1]

"Children have minds. They have imaginations. If they are told the truth in a loving and caring way, and if they are allowed to express their grief, they are capable of accepting even the most painful and devastating losses that life has to offer." —Helen Fitzgerald[2]

A developmental framework for children in grief

Under age 2	Have little understanding of death but do sense change in environment and security.
Ages 2-6	Display magical thinking: "When will they come home?"
Ages 6-9	Begin to comprehend the finality of death but often regress to magical thinking.
Ages 9-10	Acquire a more mature understanding of death and begin to appreciate its irreversibility.
Ages 11-14	Experience a budding sense of invincibility, which filters death.

Primary goals for a child griever

- Allow the child to put the event(s) into perspective.
- Allow the child to make sense of the confusion.

- Help the child begin to develop an understanding about death in general.

—Krietemeyer and Heiney[3]

Tasks facing a child in grief

- Understanding that someone has died
- Protecting the self and significant others
- Accepting and emotionally acknowledging the loss
- Bearing the pain
- Exploring and reevaluating the relationship with the deceased
- Coping with the future

—Baker, Sedney, and Gross[4]

Three issues for grieving children

- Did I cause it (death or some other loss)?
- Is it going to happen to me?
- Who is going to take care of me?

—J. William Worden[5]

Ways to be present to a grieving child

- Stop what you are doing.
- Look at the child, and listen with your eyes and ears.
- Honor the child's questions.
- Answer accurately.
- Assure the child that an adult will protect him or her.
- Avoid euphemisms: "She's asleep . . ."

"Ask your child if she is hearing any words she doesn't understand." —Helen Fitzgerald[6]

- Let a child's curiosity guide the discussion.

"No one procedure or formula will fit all children, either at the time of death or during the months that follow. Be patient, flexible and adjust to individual needs." —Alan D. Wolfelt[7]

- Ask: How much does this child want/need to know?
- Pay special attention to a child juggling multiple traumas and losses.
- Value the child's faith wonderings.
- Be alert to the sensitive child.
- Be alert to the child "taking care" of a grieving adult.
- Remember that children grieve intermittently.
- Acknowledge gaps in a child's memory.

"Children sometimes cope with loss by selectively remembering, or by reconstructing a reality in a more desirable and comfortable way." —Lynn DeSpelder and Albert Lee Strickland[8]

- Remember that children may "play" their way through bereaving.
- As much as possible maintain routines.
- Find a way creatively to commemorate the loss.

"Ask your child how she wants to remember her loved one who has died, and then help her to find ways to do this."

—Theresa Huntley[9]

- Include the child in rituals.

Ways to help a child commemorate a death

- Making a memory or treasure box
- Drawing pictures
- Having the child write a story or poem
- Planting a tree or bush
- Donating a book to the library
- Wearing an item of clothing or jewelry
- Creating a scrapbook
- Making a favorite meal
- Visiting the grave or scattering area

NOTES

1. Phyllis Rolfe Silverman, *Never Too Young to Know: Death in Children's Lives* (New York: Oxford University Press, 2000), 234.

2. Helen Fitzgerald, *The Grieving Child: A Parent's Guide* (New York: Fireside Books, 1992), 193-94.

3. B. Krietemeyer and S. P. Heiney, "Storytelling As a Therapeutic Technique in Group for School-Age Oncology Patients," *Children's Health Care* 21 (1992): 14-20.

4. John E. Baker, Mary Ann Sedney, and Esther Gross, "Psychological Tasks for Bereaved Children," *American Journal of Orthopsychiatry* 62, no. 1 (1992): 105-16.

5. J. William Worden, "Children and Grief: When a Parent Dies" (presentation at concurrent session, Fifth International Conference on Grief and Bereavement in Contemporary Society, Washington, D.C., 26 June 1997).

6. Fitzgerald, *The Grieving Child,* 44.

7. Alan D. Wolfelt, *Helping Children Cope with Grief* (Batesville, Ind.: Batesville Management Company, 1992), 5.

8. Lynn DeSpelder and Albert Lee Strickland, *The Last Dance: Encountering Death and Dying* (Boston: McGraw Hill, 2002), 361.

9. Theresa Huntley, *When Your Child Loses a Loved One* (Minneapolis: Augsburg, 2001), 49.

C. Essentials for Grief Ministry to Adolescents

An adolescent's first encounter with grief can be a life-shaping event. Sooner or later a teen will die in your church or community and teens in your congregation will be impacted. Or the teens will be impacted by the death of a youth leader or parent. I have prepared these notes to help you. How can you use them?

1. You can use this material to create a sermon addressing the death.
2. You can use this material for leading discussions with a youth minister or with those individuals who work with your teens. Do not assume that a youth minister has any preparation for dealing with an adolescent's death or grief. After a new youth minister or leader has come on board, spend some time with him or her talking about how your congregation can effectively minister to grieving teens.
3. Benjamin Franklin said, "An ounce of prevention is worth a pound of cure." Before that death happens, teach from this outline. Equip your congregation before the next school yard shooting or tragedy in your community.

WHEN IT COMES TO GRIEF, ADOLESCENTS SHOULD BE SEEN AND HEARD

"A special challenge for many bereaved adolescents is their need not to feel out of control and not to embarrass themselves in front of their peers."

—Charles A. Corr[1]

"Adolescents who are unwilling to talk to parents, counselors, or other adults may find it more congenial to address their death-related concerns in the context of a support group populated by peers with similar experiences. By establishing a community of bereaved peers, groups of this sort dispel the stigma of being 'different' or marked by a death."

—Charles A. Corr[2]

"Core issues" for adolescents

- The predictability of events
- Development of self-image
- Belonging
- A sense of fairness and justice
- Mastery and control

—J. William Worden[3]

Most common feelings discussed by grieving adolescents

- Sadness about having to cope with the actual loss of a relationship
- Feelings of excessive guilt regarding activities or deeds they wish they had or had not done with the deceased
- Anger at being left without the deceased
- Not having a chance to say good-bye
- Feeling of responsibility, that maybe if they had done something different, the person would still be with them
- Concern that the same thing may happen to them
- Overidentification with the deceased in order to maintain continuity of presence

—Beverly Raphael[4]

"Families do have a critical responsibility. But it is a responsibility shared with other individuals and organizations, such as hospices, schools, and faith communities, as well as the community at large. In times of significant loss, it is important to remember that the ability of family members to support one another can be limited."

—Kenneth Doka[5]

In assessing the impact of the death of a loved one on an adolescent

- Consider the adolescent's role in the family system or peer group before and after the death.
- Consider the nature of the relationship lost.
- Consider the remaining social and familial support network.

- Consider the adolescent's psychological maturity and coping skills at the time of the death.

—Mufson, Moreau, Weissman, and Klerman[6]

"Red flag" warning behaviors

- Suicidal thoughts or actions
- Chronic depression, sleeping difficulties, and low self-esteem
- Isolation from family and friends
- Academic failure or overachievement
- Dramatic change in personality or attitude
- Eating disorders
- Drug and alcohol abuse
- Fighting or legal troubles
- Inappropriate sexual behaviors

—Alan D. Wolfelt[7]

Primary goals for an adolescent griever

- Allow the adolescent to put the event(s) into perspective.
- Allow the adolescent to make sense of the confusion.
- Help the adolescent begin to develop an understanding about death in general.

—Krietemeyer and Heiney[8]

Ask *to whom* is the adolescent listening?

- Parent
- Counselor
- Peers
- Other pastor or youth minister/leader
- Teacher at school
- Someone in an Internet chat room

"Teenagers are fascinated with death and often spend time fantasizing about their own deaths, often to the dismay of parents."

—Helen Fitzgerald[9]

Ways to be present to a grieving adolescent

- Be available.

- Listen; don't lecture.
- Know the dangers of the "Big Man/Big Woman" Syndrome.
- Learn how to be helpful as an adolescent defines "helpful."
- Watch what you say.
- Do something practical.
- Remember the adolescent on special days.
- Stay in touch.
- Be alert to warning signals that an adolescent needs help.

—Victor Parachin[10]

- Answer accurately.
- Recognize "delay" in grieving.
- Make a place for the memory of the deceased loved one/friend in celebrating special events.

Guidelines for adults communicating about death with adolescents

- Take the lead in heightened awareness of an adolescent's concerns about death and in openness in discussing whatever he or she wishes to explore.
- Listen actively and perceptively, with special attention to the feelings that appear to underlie what the adolescent is saying.
- Accept the adolescent's feelings as real, important, and normal.
- Use supportive responses that reflect acceptance and understanding of what the adolescent is trying to say.
- Project a belief in the worth of the adolescent by resisting the temptation to solve his or her problems and by summoning an effort to help the adolescent find his or her own solutions.
- Take time to enjoy the company of the adolescent and to provide frequent opportunities for talking together.

—J. N. McNeil[11]

- Pray for and pray with the adolescent.

- Remember the grieving adolescent may numb himself or herself sexually.
- Help the adolescent find ways to commemorate his or her friend or loved one.
- Remember, the adolescent may be grieving the loss of what he or she had hoped to share in the future with the deceased.

"Bereaved adolescents may face anew their grief as their development proceeds from one developmental level to the next. This is the 'recursive aspect' of grief." —David E. Balk[12]

Critical questions to ask an adolescent griever

- Has anyone in your family died before? Who was it?
- How was the deceased important to you?
- What did this person mean to your family?
- What did you like doing with this person?
- What did you *not* like about this person?

—Allen Levine and Amanda L. Sutton[13]

Religious concerns

"Spiritual manifestations take such forms as a crisis in faith, a search for meaning, and doubt about the importance of anything."

—David E. Balk[14]

- Do you believe in God?
- Where do you think your loved one/friend went when he or she died?
- If there is a heaven, what is it like?
- What happens when someone dies?
- Will you see your loved one again?
- What did your loved one teach you?
- What gifts/talents would you like to pursue in your loved one's honor?
- Is there anything you didn't get a chance to say?

—Allen Levine and Amanda L. Sutton[15]

Questions adolescents often ask

- Survivor's guilt: Why did my sibling die and not me?
- If I am like my sibling, will my parents love me more?
- Am I "good enough" to take away my parents' grief?

—Allen Levine[16]

Family factors affecting siblings during illness and grief

- Do parents feel/believe the "wrong" child died?
- Are relatives focusing on the parents and overlooking this teen?
- Do the parents fear that something could happen to this adolescent child?
- Are the parents available for this grieving teen?
- Is there tension in the parents' marriage?
- How is the stepparent (if applicable) helping the adolescent grieve?

—Allen Levine[17]

The deceased peer does not have to be personally known—to activate the reality within an adolescent. Death has struck too close for comfort. —Harold Ivan Smith

Building a bridge into an adolescent's grief

- Find practical ways to reach out to this adolescent.
- Give the teen a tape or favorite CD.
- Take the adolescent for pizza (to a restaurant that he or she chooses).
- Rent a movie or give the teen a gift certificate for a video store.

Remembering and honoring a friend's life

An adolescent can honor by

- visiting the cemetery
- reading the friend's favorite poem or listening to his or her favorite music

- planting a tree
- visiting the family or getting together with other friends
- attending the rituals
- wearing a keepsake, an article of clothing, or a piece of jewelry
- remembering the friend on his or her birthday or a special day

—Grollman and Malikow[18]

NOTES

1. Charles A. Corr, "What Do We Know About Grieving Children and Adolescents?" in *Living with Grief: Children, Adolescents, and Loss,* ed. K. J. Doka (Philadelphia: Brunner/Mazel, 2000), 27.

2. Charles A. Corr, Clyde M. Nabe, and Donna M. Corr, *Death and Dying, Life and Living,* 2d. (Pacific Grove, Calif.: Brooks/Cole, 1997), 375.

3. J. William Worden, "Children and Grief: When a Parent Dies" (presentation at concurrent session, Fifth International Conference on Grief and Bereavement in Contemporary Society, Washington, D.C., 26 June 1997).

4. Beverly Raphael, *The Anatomy of Bereavement* (New York: Basic, 1983), 139-76.

5. Kenneth Doka, "Eight Myths About Children, Adolescents, and Loss," in *Living with Grief: Children, Adolescents, and Loss,* ed. K. J. Doka (Philadelphia: Brunner/Mazel, 2000), 34.

6. L. Mufson, D. Moreau, M. M. Weissman, and G. L. Klerman, *Interpersonal Psychotherapy for Depressed Adolescents* (New York: Guilford, 1993), 90-91.

7. Alan D. Wolfelt, *Healing the Bereaved Child: Grief Gardening, Growth Through Grief, and Other Touchstones for Caregivers* (Fort Collins, Colo.: Companion Press, 1996), 281-82.

8. B. Krietemeyer and S. P. Heiney, "Storytelling as a Therapeutic Technique in Group for School-Age Oncology Patients," *Children's Health Care* 21 (1992): 14-20.

9. Helen Fitzgerald, *The Grieving Child: A Parent's Guide* (New York: Fireside Books, 1992), 57.

10. Victor Parachin, "How to Help a Grieving Teenager," *Director* 70 (May 1998): 14, 16.

11. J. N. McNeil, "Talking About Death: Adolescents, Parents, and Peers," in *Adolescence and Death,* ed. C. A. Corr and J. N. McNeil (New York: Springer, 1986), 185-201.

12. David E. Balk, in *Living with Grief: Children, Adolescents, and Loss,* ed. K. J. Doka (Philadelphia: Brunner/Mazel, 2000), 43.

13. Allen Levine and Amanda L. Sutton, "Breaking the Silence: Learning to Decode the Disenfranchised Grief of Adolescents" (presentation at Association for Death Education and Counseling, Toronto, March 29, 2001).

14. Balk, *Living with Grief: Children, Adolescents, and Loss,* 39.

15. Levine, "Breaking the Silence."

16. Ibid.

17. Ibid.

18. Earl A. Grollman and Max Malikow, *Living When a Young Friend Commits Suicide* (Boston: Beacon Press, 1999), 56.

2
LETTERS

▶ "You've got mail." The phrase is a watchword in contemporary society. Nearly 2,000 years ago in the Early Church, congregations eagerly received letters from the apostle Paul. Letters made a difference then; they make a difference now. God still works through letters—particularly well-crafted letters. Unfortunately, letter writing is something of a lost art in an e-mail society.

After suffering a stroke, actor Kirk Douglas was not at all certain that he could say more than "Thank you" during his appearance on the Academy Awards to accept a lifetime achievement award. In *My Stroke of Luck,* Douglas writes about the impact of the outpouring of letters, faxes, and phone calls that followed:

> One letter startled me. It was from King Hussein, the ruler of Jordan. He was one of the billions watching the Oscar show. He invited me to visit him in Jordan and see the country.
>
> Of course, I couldn't make such a long trip, but I thanked him for his kindness. I needed it. His letter encouraged me to work harder with my speech therapist, exercise more, and talk with other people besides my family.

Soon after sending the letter, King Hussein died. Douglas lamented, "He would never know how much his letter helped me" (89-90).

Admittedly, you may never know how much a letter means to a griever. In God's economy of timing, your words could make a big difference.

Some pastors find writing a note, card, or letter to a griever a difficult assignment. What can a pastor write that will be helpful—that will show a pastor cares? The letters, whose images follow, will be jump starters for some of the letters you will from time to time write and send. Look at the images, choose the letter(s) you want, and then access the CD for revising and printing.

You are free to use the letter or to lift sentences of paragraphs from different letters to create a letter for a specific occasion. Some pastors will find just reading through a couple of the letters will ignite the creative juices.

Let God use you to minister through a letter that can be read, reread, and treasured for years to come.

It would be wise to keep a record of the letters you send. Otherwise, a griever might receive a letter and have a feeling of "Oh, it's a form letter." That could be quite counterproductive.

Letters

Letter 1

May God who walked the dusty road
to Emmaus with grievers
bend low to you
these grief-filled days.

May your path frequently lead
to that oasis called courage.

May your eyesight rest on a closer horizon
colored with hope.

May you never lose trust
in God's incredible mercy,
new every morning,
sufficient for the demands
of any day.

Letter 2

Letter for the Parent(s) After the Death of a Child

[Date]

[Name]
[Address]

Dear [Name(s)]:

In moments like this I struggle for words that could begin to comfort you in the loss of [your daughter/son or Name]. In losses like this even the best-intended words fail to convey what we feel. I have not lost a child. I do not know what you are experiencing, but God does know.

In 1921, a young couple in Maryland lost a three-year-old son just after Christmas. The loss was devastating. Yet neither one expected to "get over it." Years later, Dwight Eisenhower counseled another grieving father, "Don't expect to get over it." Grief for a child is a lifelong responsibility.

How blessed [Name] was to have you for (a) parent(s). Three millennia ago, King David lost several children, one just a baby. He wrote, "I will go to him, for he will not return to me" (2 Sam. 12:23). God will take loving care of your baby and of you.

You are in my thoughts and prayers. I will intentionally pray for you. This community of faith prays for you and wants to stand with you in this time of great loss.

An out-of-order death like this leaves all of us wondering *why*. Jesus knows this word, because He, too, asked, "Why have you forsaken me?" (Mark 15:34). As your pastor, I wish I could offer some reason why this has happened. I have no idea why. I can only come alongside you and walk with you through this nightmare called grief.

May God give you strength sufficient for the demands of these days.

[Pastor's Name]

Letter 3

Letter to a Couple for a Perinatal Loss

[Date]

[Name]

[Address]

Dear [Names]:

In moments like this pastors struggle to find words that might comfort and not offend. We're supposed to have the right words at our disposal. Not today.

How you wanted this baby. What great parents you would have made!

It will be tempting to find ways to hide your pain from each other as well as from family and friends. Well-meaning people will bombard you with hackneyed clichés. At times, silence will wound. You will experience heart-wrenching moments when your attention goes to babies in the arms of others rather than yours.

At times, it will be difficult to understand God's intention in all of this. Go ahead and ask all of your *why* questions. But also ask God, "Now what?"

A brokenhearted man wrote words that have brought comfort to many. "What a Friend we have in Jesus, / All our sins *and griefs* to bear! / What a privilege to carry / Ev'rything to God in prayer!"* Everything? Everything.

Tell God whatever is on your heart.

Give me opportunities to be a pastor to you in these difficult days.

[Pastor's Name]

*Joseph M. Scriven (*Sing to the Lord*, 625; emphasis added.)

Letter 4

Letter to a Father After the Death of a Child

[Date]

[Name]

[Address]

Dear [Name]:

Thomas Paine wrote in 1776, "These are the times that try men's souls." As I have thought about you and prayed for you, I have developed a new appreciation for Paine's insight. Grief is a soul-trying experience. To have to live with this significant loss without becoming bitter will be one of life's most demanding challenges.

Perhaps someone has already asked you, "How's your wife?" Sometimes people seem to focus on the mother's loss and ignore the father's grief. No doubt someone has already suggested that you need to be "strong" for your wife. If only there were a bumper sticker or T-shirt with the message "Dads grieve too!"

When I see you, I intend to deliberately ask, "How are *you*?" I hope you will tell me.

The loss of a child and of your dreams for that child can be difficult on a marriage. I pray that you will each be able to honor the loss of *this* child. There may be other children, but no one will take the place of [Name].

Three millennia ago, David became a perinatal griever. He wrote sobering words, "Can I bring him back again? I will go to him, but he will not return to me" (2 Sam. 12:23).

Honor your grief.
Share that grief with your spouse [and children].
Trust the God who knows your name is [Name].
Give your wife some space to do her grief work.
Tell me ways, as your pastor, that I can be a companion to you in these difficult days.

May God--the Source of all comfort--give you comfort.

[Pastor's Name]

Letter 5

Letter to Someone Grieving an Elderly Parent

[Date]

[Name]

[Address]

Dear [Name]:

The Scripture says, "Precious in the sight of the LORD is the death of his saints" (Ps. 116:15). In this culture, we tend to minimize the pain of those who grieve for an elderly parent. "He lived his life" and "she lived a good life" are common clichés people think will comfort.

The death of a parent can be an eye-opening experience. Eternity takes on a new intensity. Some adults feel more vulnerable with the death of a parent.

Grief cannot be prorated. Give your grief for your aged [mother/father] its voice. Spend some time with your memories. Grief has lessons to teach us as we are willing to learn.

May God's peace be with you this day.

[Pastor's Name]

Letter 6

Death by Suicide

[Date]

[Name]

[Address]

Dear [Name]:

My heart goes out to you in the loss of [Name]. Such a tragic death leaves so many unanswered questions. *Why* is often punctuated with exclamation marks rather than a question mark. I cannot begin to comprehend the ache in your heart.

Go ahead and ask your questions. Reginald Johnson says, "God never chides his children for being children." God realizes you do not--cannot--understand what led to this tragic decision. In my experience as a pastor, rarely do we get answers to our *why* questions. However, if we ask "Now what?" God helps us discover hope.

Many who have grieved this particular loss have turned to the Scriptures. Seize this promise of God: "Never will I leave you; never will I forsake you" (Heb. 13:5).

I will be calling you from time to time. As your pastor and friend, I want to continue to walk with you on this grief path.

You are in my prayers and in the prayers of this community of faith.

[Pastor's Name]

Letter 7

Letter for a Spouse's Death

[Date]

[Name]

[Address]

Dear [Name]:

You have come to my heart this morning. Please accept my heartfelt condolences on the death of your spouse, [Name]. Years ago you made a promise, "Till death us do part." Now that reality has come. It would be easy to dodge such commitments; in our world, many do. But you worked hard to make your marriage a blessing not only to yourselves but also to your children, your community, and this community of faith.

You ask, "How do I live without [Name]?" I offer only one suggestion. Looking down through time and saying "I will have to spend the next 30 years without [Name]" would feel like a slap to the heart. I would suggest you refocus and look to the immediate future. "How will I live *this* day, *this* week, *this* month without [Name]?" God gives us grace to deal with life's tragedies one day at a time. The Israelites had to rely on manna, a day at a time.

Please know that you are in my thoughts and prayers. As your pastor I want to be available to help you on this grief path. Please know that this church lifts you to God's heart.

[Pastor's Name]

Letter 8

Letter for a Second Loss

[Date]

[Name]

[Address]

Dear [Name]:

Your pastor is at a loss for words. I cannot believe that just a few weeks ago I sat composing a letter to you after [Name's] death--now [Second Name's] death. I am pondering what to say to comfort you in this new loss. No doubt you have heard lots of clichés and "words of wisdom" from well-meaning people. I will not add to those.

In the letter of Paul to the Philippians, he says that God spared his friend Epaphroditus from death "to spare me sorrow upon sorrow" (2:27). That phrase sounds odd in light of your loss. Why now? Why [Second Name]? Why has God allowed you [Names of Family Members Impacted by the Death] another sorrow?

We may never understand the timing of [Second Name's] death. Some losses are so unexplainable that a person cannot "hold up" under them without God's care and the care of God's people.

People will suggest to you, "God never puts more on us than we can bear." In your case, I am not sure. I do believe that God will help you bear up under this load of loss.

I hope you will always talk about [Second Name]; that you will find ways to honor [his/her] memory; and that when you start to say "[Second Name] would have loved this," you will go ahead and say it even if it makes others uncomfortable.

I hope that you will always treasure [Second Name's] love for you.

I hope that you will always bring your grief to God.

Please know that I am praying for you.

[Pastor's Name]

Letter 9

Letter on a Holiday or Significant Day in the Griever's Life

[Date]

[Name]

[Address]

Dear [Name]:

This will be a first [identify occasion] not to have [Name or Title (Mom, etc.)] ready to [blow out the candles and] open presents. [Or to enjoy her hospitality, etc.]

I hope this day the memory of [Name or Title] will comfort you. What a remarkable [man/woman/young man/young woman/teen/child].

I am praying that God will be close to you in this day [or season] and that He will bring you a fresh awareness of His grace.

You are being thought about *today*.

[Pastor's Name]

Letter 10

Letter on a Birthday

[Date]

[Name]

[Address]

Dear [Name]:

It seems odd to look at my birthday list and see a name for which I will not mail a card. It seems hard to believe that [Name] died this year. There are lots of other terms and phrases, but the reality is nevertheless the same.

I cannot begin to appreciate what must be going through your heart and mind, having enjoyed so many birthdays with [Name]. I know that you will be grateful that you had a chance to love [him/her] and receive [his/her] love. The world is a better place because [Name] lived in this community and was part of our [congregation/fellowship].

I am thankful for having known [Name], for all the encouragement and ideas [he/she] offered me, and for the meals and moments we shared. So many good memories come to my mind.

[I am grateful that he/she allowed me to witness his/her courage through the dying.]

I am not certain how our loved ones celebrate birthdays in heaven, but I believe they do. Perhaps every day is a birthday in heaven.

Please know that you are in my prayers on this red-letter day of your heart's calendar. My life is blessed by knowing you.

May good memories and God's grace be presents opened in your heart.

[Pastor's Name]

Letter 11

Letter for an Expected Loss

[Date]

[Name]

[Address]

Dear [Name]:

Sometimes, there is little one can say
when death has again touched a life, a family,
and when the anchor points
have again been rearranged.

No magic words, no clichés,
even from a pastor or friend,
alter the reality of the death of [Name].
Life has again changed.

Yet in our losses, it is natural to wonder
what more we could have done.
The "If only I had . . .'s" can torment
a soul raw with grief.

May God remind you
of His greatest promise:
There is another land beyond the wide river.
And in that land we are free to be
those uniquely creative beings God wills us to be.

If you listen closely in your sadness,
loss, and wonderment,
you may catch a glimpse of the sounds
of the celebration
God calls eternity.

[Pastor's Name]

Letter 12

Note for Difficult Times

[Date]

[Name]

[Address]

Dear [Name]:

I have no idea what it feels like
these tough days
to be [Recipient's Name].

God does.

May God who loves you
give you strength
more than sufficient
for the demands of [this day/these days.]

May God who loves you
bring friends to help you carry this grief.

May God who loves you
bless you and keep you, and
may He turn His face toward you
and give you peace--*
great unfathomable peace.

[Pastor's Name]

*See Num. 6:24, 26.

Letter 13

Note for Caregiver After Death

[Name],
for all you've been through,
suffered,
endured,
struggled with,
survived,
you, [Name],
courageous [lady/gentleman],
child of God,
deserve
recognition
for your loving, faithful care to [Deceased's Name]
during [his/her illness/hospitalization(s)].

Not everyone is blessed to have had
such a caregiver.

May God bring comfort to you
and replenish your strength.
May God point you toward the future
He plans for you.

[Pastor's Name]

"Then you will call upon me and come and pray to me, and I will listen to you" (Jer. 29:12).

Letter 14

Letter for a Death

[Date]

[Name]

[Address]

Dear [Name]:

I just learned of the death of [Name or your (relationship title--mom, etc.)] and wanted to write and express my sympathy. I do not have words that will take away the pain you feel. But I do know that God pays close attention to those who have loved and lost. And He will certainly pay attention to you and to all who have been touched by [Name's] death.

I counsel those who have been touched by loss to "give your grief its voice." Unfortunately, as you already know, we live in a culture that will urge you to "get over it" or to "get on with life," or to "make the most of it." Unfortunately, we offer tired clichés when we don't know what to say.

I want you to know that I am praying that God will be close to you, that He will give you strength for the realities of these days, and that He will give you courage for the toughest task that comes your way.

A brokenhearted, widowed Jackie Kennedy wrote to friends soon after President Kennedy was assassinated: "I consider my life to be over, and I will spend the rest of my life waiting for it really to be over."

But good days came to Jackie, three more decades of good days. Good things, which in the early days of her grief, she could not have anticipated. I am praying that there will be--in time--good days for you too.

You have made a difference in my life and in so many lives.

[Pastor's Name]

Letter 15
Letter When Life Ambushes Us

[Date]

[Name]

[Address]

Dear [Name]:

Life never shields us from
the ambush, the surprise, the unexpected, does it?

Yet God promises to be with us
in the unimaginable, unfathomable moments
when things seem to have gone terribly wrong, and
when the "way it is supposed to be"
seems turned upside down.

Sometimes
a griever needs a companion--
someone who has "been there"
or has been down a familiar
stretch of the landscape of the heart--
Someone whose heart, too, has been lacerated
in a strikingly similar way.

Perhaps through a fellow griever's words
or a fellow griever's attempt to
find words to capture the loss,
you may hear the soft whisper of grace
and encounter the God who loves you
in a fresh, new way.

Remember,
[Name] is not gone until
two things happen:
You stop saying [his/her] name, [Name], and
You stop telling stories about [him/her].

[Pastor's Name]

Letter 16
Death of a Father

[Date]

[Name]

[Address]

Dear [Name]:

In the passing of a father
we taste
a once-in-a-lifetime experience.
There will be other deaths,
other griefs--
but only one passing of a father.
Somehow, we are never really ready
for all of the realities, the complications,
the implications.

In your time of loss,
I hope you will give grief its voice.
Your "griefprint" will be as individual
as your thumbprint.
Listen to your heart and your life's wisdom.

Please know that you are in my prayers
and in my thoughts
in these difficult days of loss.

[Pastor's Name]

Letter 17
Letter to a Mother

[Date]

[Name]

[Address]

Dear [Name]:

I cannot begin to imagine all the weight that must be on your shoulders and also upon your heart. Across the years, I have listened to many mothers try to find words to wrap around their pain and grief. A child is not supposed to die first--just not supposed to. I believe that some of the pain you now know is what Mary experienced that Good Friday as Jesus died.

I have been amazed by the words of Joseph Scriven, who wrote the hymn "What a Friend We Have in Jesus." We all know the phrase "All our sins and griefs to bear." What we often hear is "All our sins . . . to bear." But Scriven deliberately included "and griefs" because he knew about grief. Twice he had fiancés die--one the day before the wedding.

Please know that I am praying that God will be close to you in these early days of sorrow. I pray that the One who brought comfort to the two grievers on the road to Emmaus will find ways to bring you comfort.

[Pastor's Name]

Letter 18
Griever Uncertain of Deceased's Salvation

[Date]

[Name]

[Address]

Dear [Name]:

I have been thinking about the questions you asked following [Name's] memorial service. I have also been thinking of these words in John: "For God so loved the world that he gave his one and only Son, that whoever believes in him shall not perish but have eternal life" (3:16). God's "whoever" is outrageously extravagant.

No one, this side of eternity, can say with certainty who "made it" or did not make it. Heaven will have its surprises.

So we must commit [Name] to the God who loves [him/her]. We can trust that God will be good to [him/her]. Scripture is clear that it is not God's will that anyone perish (see 2 Pet. 3:9).

In the moments when these questions weigh heavy on your heart, I urge you to again place [Name] in God's hands.

May God bring you peace in this significant loss.

[Pastor's Name]

Letter 19

Heavenly Father,

We commit [Name] to You.

We have not "lost" [Name] by [his/her] home-going to the place You have prepared for all who love You.

[Name] now experiences what [he/she] has so long trusted. [He/She] has discovered the reality of the resurrection You promised.

Give [Name of Recipient] strength to grieve. Turn Your face toward [him/her], and may [he/she] know the comfort of Your peace, a peace that the world cannot understand in such moments.

And when the grief hurts and [Name of Recipient] aches, God of all comfort, pay attention, to Your servants who must now live in a world reordered by death's touch.

Give [Name/Names] great wisdom to explain death to those young minds You have entrusted to [him/her/them].

Remind us that we are an Easter people, en route to the home You have prepared for us.
Amen.

[Pastor's Name]

Letter 20
Letter to a Friend of the Deceased

[Date]

[Name]

[Address]

Dear [Name]:

I wanted to take a moment and write you following the death of your friend [Name]. What a friend you were to [him/her]. [Name/Your (relationship title)] has shared stories of your devoted friendship. I can only begin to imagine the sense of loss you are experiencing.

In my work with grievers, I remind them of the words of Victoria Alexander after the death of her father. She says that every griever has three needs:

- To try to find words for the loss
- To say the words aloud
- To know that the words have been heard

Unfortunately, our society doesn't always recognize that friends grieve too. Yet scripture chronicles David's lament for his fallen friend, Jonathan. "I grieve for you, Jonathan my brother, you were very dear to me" (2 Sam. 1:26). And the shortest verse in the Bible, "Jesus wept" (John 11:35), is about Jesus' grief for Lazarus.

It is critical that all grievers, especially the friends, find ways to give grief its voice.

May you find comfort in the memories of [Name] and your friendship.

I pray that God will find ways to remind you of His comfort.

[Pastor's Name]

Letter 21

Letter on the Anniversary of a Death/Memorial Service

[Date]

[Name]

[Address]

Dear [Name]:
The calendar for most people
merely says [date of death/service].

But for you
and for all those
who loved [Name]
and for those into whose lives
[Name] brought so much joy,
this is a special day in the heart.

I cannot begin to imagine
how much you must miss [Name].

But I was reminded,
seeing *Shadowlands* again,
of C. S. Lewis's words:
"Why love . . .
if losing hurts so much?
I have no answers
except the life I have lived."

You know well
that not every [sister/brother/cousin/etc.]
has experienced such love.
So today find a moment
to celebrate that wonderful,
wonderful love.

[Pastor's Name]

Letter 22

Letter to a Mother upon Late Notification of a Child's Death

[Date]

[Name]

[Address]

Dear [Name]:

Unfortunately, I just learned of [Name's] death. I am saddened by your loss. I am almost at a loss for words that might comfort you. I am sure that many have stepped into this darkness to offer you words of comfort and assurance.

I can only begin to imagine what you must have experienced and must now be experiencing.

Certainly, you have grieved for [Name]. But this will be a different grief--a mother's grief. How many mothers have protested, "But a child isn't supposed to die first. I was." So I hope in your grieving you will notice the words that slip into your mind and heart.

Please know that you will be in my prayers. I pray that God will be graciously tender to you.

People of the Jewish faith recite the griever's kaddish for 11 months. Many Christians find great meaning in the words, especially the last segment, "May the creator of heavenly peace bestow peace on us."

I pray that the Creator of heavenly peace will, in time, bring you peace.

Give your grief its voice.

[Pastor's Name]

Letter 23
Letter at Some Difficult Point in First Year

[Date]

[Name]

[Address]

Dear [Name]:

Loss does not end on any neat schedule.

Long after others have stopped mentioning the loss, we begin to comprehend its depth. Most often we are reminded in stray moments.

May this day be a day to revisit the memories of [Name or your mother, etc.].

May this be a day to honor the freshness of grief.

May this day be a recognition of the blessing of having had [Name] for a [mother/father/brother/sister/son/daughter].

May God who has a tender spot for those who grieve be close to you today.

[Pastor's Name]

Letter 24
Letter with Prayer for Grace in a Situation

[Date]

[Name]

[Address]

A Prayer for [Name]

Kind Lord
in the demands of this day,
known and unknown,
be with [Name].

Give [Name]
in this time of grief
the strength and courage
and a grace grit
to answer
those demands,
confident
that You will not
ask more
than [he/she] can give.

And remind those who care for [Name]
of ways we can reach out to [him/her].
Amen.

[Pastor's Name]

Letter 25
General Letter to a Griever

[Date]

[Name]

[Address]

Dear [Name]:

I wanted you to know that you have been and will continue to be in my thoughts as you do thoroughly grieve for your [relationship title]. We live in a "grief lite" culture, so those who grieve really do stand out in a crowd.

Victoria Alexander says that all grievers have three needs: to find words for the loss, to say the words aloud, and to know that those words have been heard.

And [Name], in case anyone from the "grief patrol" should be rude enough to tell you that you are *not* doing grief work correctly, I hope you will take a long look at your thumb. Because out of 6 billion people on planet Earth your thumbprint is one of a kind! If God went to so much trouble to make your thumbprint unique, why would your "griefprint" not be unique as well?

The grief patrol will ask, "How old was your [relationship]?" (When you tell them, they respond, "Oh, well then, [he/she] lived a good long life.") Then they ask, "Was [he/she] a Christian?" (When you say yes, they will say, "Oh, well then, [he's/she's] in heaven.") The grief patrol is made of lots of Barney Fifes who cannot let grief happen. But their questions hang around long after the questioners have moved on.

Your [relationship title] gave the world a precious gift in [Name of Recipient]. May you find comfort in [his/her] love and life. May you find a way to long remember [him/her]. May you grieve in such a way that others will find courage also to do *thorough* grief work. [He/She] is not "gone" until you stop saying [his/her] name and telling stories about [him/her].

If I can be of any help, please call on me.

[Pastor's Name]

Letter 26
Letter on Death of a Son/Daughter

[Date]

[Name]

[Address]

To my friend, [Name]:

I will not say, "I know what you are going through."
Because you would say, "Is pastor nuts!
    [He/She] doesn't know what I am going through
    with the loss of [my son/daughter or Name]!
    How could [he/she]!"
But I do have this Friend who does know what my friend
    is experiencing, cause He lost a Son too.
So I will just remind Him--a lot--
    to be close to you,
    to "hang out" near you and with you
    as you try on this new loss.

And I will pray that He will bring into your life
    special people
    who will understand [son/daughter] grief.

And I will pray that He will give you great grace
    for those inevitable moments
    when people say really stupid things
    or when people say nothing
    and the silence stings.

And I pray that He will bring you great memories
    of the 1,001 ways you kindly and faithfully
    shared with your [son/daughter].

And I pray that He will bring you great peace.

As I say to grievers, "Give your unique grief its voice."

[Pastor's Name]

Letter 27
Letter to a Grandparent

[Date]

[Name]
[Address]

Dear [Name]:

Words are inadequate in responding to the death of a grandchild [or Name of Child]. I wish I could craft a sentence or a phrase that could begin to ease the ache. These words from a wonderful hymn writer speak to the demands on a griever's heart: "And grace to live the questions now--until your answers come" (Edith Downing).

Former First Lady Claudia "Lady Bird" Johnson rightly said, "People must be given the opportunity to hurt out loud."

I think that we need opportunities to live out our questions out loud too.

To have to say "Hello" and "Good-bye" at the same time is one of life's most demanding assignments. Moreover, the grandparent not only grieves for [himself/herself] but also for the child.

May God comfort you and all your family. May He bring you strength sufficient for the demands of every day.

[Pastor's Name]

Letter 28
Letter on Third-Month Anniversary

[Date]

[Name]
[Address]

Dear [Name]:

Three months have passed since [Name]'s death. No doubt it still seems like yesterday.

Many people live expecting that one day an answer will come for the "Why?" "Why [him/her]?" "Why now?" questions that plague grievers.

I wanted to share some thoughts on why from Frederica Mathewes-Green: "The only useful question in such a time is not 'Why?' but 'What's next?' What should I do next? What should be my response to this ugly event? How can I bring the best out of it? How can God bring resurrection out of it?"

God does not expect us to find answers on our own.

The psalmist says that God "lifts the needy from the ash heap" (Ps. 113:7). At the risk of sounding outrageous, I want to express my belief that out of the ashes of your loss, something good will emerge. God does not want you to waste the pain. God wants to help you discover that good.

I would like to come sit down with you and explore the ways we can keep [Name]'s name alive. Like you, I do not want [Name] to be forgotten.

[Pastor's Name]

Letter 29

Letter About Returning to Church

[Date]

[Name]

[Address]

Dear [Name]:

Like many grievers, returning to church after a loss may be difficult for you--particularly when it's where the funeral was held. Yet some grievers have great experiences, while others have difficult, even hurtful, ones. A lot of our people will not know what to say to you. They will offer you more clichés to go along with those you've heard. Some will be afraid of saying the wrong thing, so they say nothing. Some will quote Rom. 8:28, expecting the promise of those words to comfort you. We all mean well. Few of us know what to say until we have spent time on the grief path.

As a pastor who loves you, I want you to know that I am praying that God will guide you in making this decision. I am sure there are memories of [Name] all over this church. Although I do not sit with my spouse for the services, I can only begin to imagine how it will be for you to sit alone.

I will understand if you do not feel up to coming to church for a while. I will understand if you are here next Sunday. I will understand if you come late or leave early. I will understand if you cry. This is God's house--you do not have to feel "strong" here.

Scripture reports that after the death of Bathsheba and David's sons, David "went into the house of the LORD and worshiped" (2 Sam. 12:20). I believe the last word is the most significant: David *worshiped* in his great grief.

Some amazing words in scripture are found in Job. Job was so vulnerable in saying to his friends, "What I feared has come upon me; what I dreaded has happened to me" (3:25). Those who had sat with him in silence felt the need to admonish their friend. "Then Eliphaz the Temanite replied: . . . " (4:1ff.). By speaking, Eliphaz lost the chance to be one of the greatest comforters of all time. Job finally challenged these would-be comforters, "Do you mean to . . . treat the words of a despairing man as wind?" (6:26).

You may recall the words of that old chorus, "Lord, lay some soul upon my heart . . . and love that soul through me." Even as your pastor, I worry that somehow my words will sound less than comforting to you. I hope you will tell me if they do.

Even though you may not be here this Sunday, you will be in our hearts. And we will pray that God will be close to you.

[Pastor's Name]

Letter 30

Letter for Memorial Day

[Date]

[Name]
[Address]

Dear [Name]:

Memorial Day
takes on a whole new meaning
when we have buried a loved one.

I am coming to believe
that memories
are little rehearsals
for resurrection.

May the God who loves you
be close
on this first Memorial Day.

May you be reminded of the love you shared,
the children you gave the world,
and the hope of seeing [Name] again.

[Pastor's Name]

3
RESOURCES*

The nine resources in this chapter can be used in a variety of ways:

1. These resources will be used in meetings of the mutual-help groups. The most appropriate use will be mentioned in the leader's notes.
2. These resources can be used in grief counseling. For example, you might share Resource 2, "Rights for Grievers," at the start of a session with a griever. Ask the griever to read through the list. Then ask, "Which one leaps out at you?" or "Which one grabs your attention?"

   Or you could give the sheet and ask the griever to read and reflect on the list before the next session.
3. Individual resources can be sent with letters or cards of affirmation. One of the resources might persuade an individual to seek grief counseling.
4. Resources 5, 6, 7, and 8 can be used in family conferences to gather thoughts to use in the funeral or memorial service, especially when the memorial service is scheduled at a later date.

---

*Printable versions of these resources are included on *The Grief Care Kit* CD.

Resource 1

Over the years one resource that has proved helpful to grievers is this simple Permission to Mourn form. We grieve in a "Get over it!" and "Move on!" world. Rarely do we say, "Grieve!" There are several ways this form can be used effectively.

In the mutual-help group, you may want to hand out the permission forms in the first meeting of the group. If a person chooses not to come back, he or she will still have been encouraged to grieve.

You may want to share a permission form with a counselee. When you do, offer a prayer: "God, would You give [Name] permission to grieve this significant loss [he/she] has experienced. You do not take away our grief. You come to *accompany* us in the valley of the shadow. Remind [Name] that Your grace will be sufficient for the demands of the season called grief."

Ask the griever to carry the permission form in his or her wallet, billfold, purse, or briefcase or to place it where he or she can frequently see it.

Be prepared for grievers to ask for copies to share with other family members.

One of the most important responsibilities of a pastor in this day is to give people permission to grieve—to grieve thoroughly.

Permission to Mourn

The holder of this certificate, ____________________, is hereby entitled to publicly acknowledge his or her loss, to mourn openly, to share narratives of the loss, and to recruit social support in his or her own way and time, without apology or embarrassment.

Tears, memories, silence, uncertainty, and strong emotions are hereby enfranchised.

Please treat this griever with kindness, compassion, and love.

This certificate has no expiration date.

Resource 2

RIGHTS FOR GRIEVERS

1. I have the right to experience my own unique grief.
2. I have the right to talk about my grief.
3. I have the right to feel a multitude of emotions.
4. I have the right to be tolerant of my physical and emotional and financial limits.
5. I have the right to experience "griefbursts."
6. I have the right to make use of additional ritual.
7. I have the right to embrace my spirituality.
8. I have the right to search for meaning.
9. I have the right to honor my memories.
10. I have the right to move toward my grief and to heal.

—Adapted from Alan D. Wolfelt,
The Journey Through Grief: Reflections on Healing, 141-43.

Resource 3

PUTTING MY GRIEF INTO WORDS

"To be able to put into words and phrases what others only think is what makes poets and sages!" —Sidney Jourard

Take the suggested phrase and write a poem. You may choose to have lines rhyme or not rhyme. Be creative. There is *no* way you can mess this up!

Grief came knocking at my door one day

____

____

____

____

____

I keep hoping that one of these days

____

____

____

____

____

Resource 4

AN ACT OF GRATITUDE

If grievers only focus on what has been lost, they miss the blessing of recognizing what remains. Our expressions of gratitude can be given for small items, things we once took for granted, or for those people who are companioning us on this painful journey. Gratitude audits are essential to doing thorough grief work.

On this sheet list a dozen "gratitudes."

Today/Tonight I am grateful for ______________________________.

Today/Tonight I am grateful for ______________________________.

Today/Tonight I am grateful for ______________________________.

Today/Tonight I am grateful for ______________________________.

Today/Tonight I am grateful for ______________________________.

Today/Tonight I am grateful for ______________________________.

Today/Tonight I am grateful for ______________________________.

Today/Tonight I am grateful for ______________________________.

Today/Tonight I am grateful for ______________________________.

Today/Tonight I am grateful for ______________________________.

Today/Tonight I am grateful for ______________________________.

Today/Tonight I am grateful for ______________________________.

Resource 5

ACROSTICS AS EULOGIES

Acrostics have long been a way that individuals wrote eulogies. If you had to describe your loved one's characteristics—positive and negative—using the ABC's, what would you include? Be honest! In the Jewish tradition *hesped* is a balanced eulogy that acknowledges the good as well as the bad. A false eulogy impedes reconciliation with the loss.

A	__________	N	__________
B	__________	O	__________
C	__________	P	__________
D	__________	Q	__________
E	__________	R	__________
F	__________	S	__________
G	__________	T	__________
H	__________	U	__________
I	__________	V	__________
J	__________	W	__________
K	__________	X	__________
L	__________	Y	__________
M	__________	Z	__________

Resource 6

THINGS I WANT TO REMEMBER AND REMEMBER TO FORGET

Healing and reconciling are not about forgetting. Reconciling our grief is about remembering and sometimes about remembering to forget. On this page list the things you want to remember and the things you want to forget.

I will always want to remember ______________________.

I need to remember to forget ______________________.

I will always want to remember ______________________.

I need to remember to forget ______________________.

I will always want to remember ______________________.

I need to remember to forget ______________________.

I will always want to remember ______________________.

I need to remember to forget ______________________.

I will always want to remember ______________________.

I need to remember to forget ______________________.

I will always want to remember ______________________.

I need to remember to forget ______________________.

I will always want to remember ______________________.

I need to remember to forget ______________________.

Resource 7

A EULOGY FOR MY LOVED ONE

"There is no statute of limitations on a eulogy. The eulogy should not be a glossy finish or a whitewash for a complex and colorful life. Nor should a eulogy be confused with an obituary. A eulogy should be words to portray as accurately and lovingly as possible the measure of a person's depths."

—Marc Gafni, *Soul Prints: Your Path to Fulfillment* (New York: Pocket Books, 2001), 110.

Here's what I want you to know about my loved one:

Resource 8

A DOZEN THINGS I WANT TO REMEMBER ABOUT MY LOVED ONE

"Nothing can make up for the absence of someone we loved, and it would be wrong to try to find a substitute; we must simply hold out and see it through. That sounds very hard at first, but at the same time it is a great consolation, for the gap, as long as it remains unfilled, preserves the bonds between us. It is nonsense to say that God fills the gap; he does not fill it, but on the contrary, keeps it empty and so helps us keep alive our former communion with each other, either at the cost of pain."

—Dietrich Bonhoeffer, *Letters and Papers from Prison,* ed. Eberhard Bethge, rev. ed. (New York: Macmillan, 1967), 200.

1. ________________________
2. ________________________
3. ________________________
4. ________________________
5. ________________________
6. ________________________
7. ________________________
8. ________________________
9. ________________________
10. ________________________
11. ________________________
12. ________________________

Resource 9

GUIDELINES FOR GROUP PARTICIPATION

This mutual-help grief group has some shared assumptions

- ☐ *Grief and loss are a vital part of being alive.* If you love, sooner or later you will lose and you will grieve.
- ☐ *Sharing leads to reconciliation.* Grief is a lot like a complicated jigsaw puzzle. In reality, another griever in the group may possess a "missing piece" to your puzzle. Listening is not about accepting everything but about offering hospitality to the one who is sharing. You will be asked to listen with your ears, eyes, and your heart.
- ☐ *A griever needs a* mekom hanekhama*—the Hebrew for "a safe place to grieve."* By this point you have probably already experienced "interrupters" who attempt to discount or short-circuit an honest expression of grief: "Oh, you shouldn't feel that way" (which sounds like being scolded). Rarely do grievers have persons who offer the gracious hospitality of hearing them all the way to the ends of their sentences without wanting to "fix" them.
- ☐ *Each griever has a story to tell and a narrative that needs to be told and to be heard.* The story is more than "just the facts." The story is about how we interpret the facts and how we live with those facts.
- ☐ *Answers and explanations are rare.* In a scientific world the cause of death may, in many cases, remain a mystery. J. William Worden says that learning to live without answers is the difficult task facing grievers. (J. William Worden, *Grief Counseling and Grief Therapy: A Handbook for the Mental Health Practitioner,* 2d ed. [New York: Springer, 1991], 16.)
- ☐ *Narratives contain unanswerable yet need-to-be-asked questions.* One father in exasperation responded to his sons, "Why do you ask so many questions?" The child answered without hesitation, "How do you expect me to learn if I don't ask questions." Grievers need safe spaces to try out and live out questions.

A mutual-help grief group is *not*

- ☐ *a therapy group*—although it will be therapeutic. Many grievers do not need a therapist—but do need safe spaces, safe places, and safe faces.
- ☐ *a group that pop-psychologizes grievers:* "You know what your problem is? We'll tell you!"
- ☐ *an ongoing group that meets indefinitely.* This group will meet for six or seven weeks, although some groups may continue longer.
- ☐ *a place to find easy answers.* Answers are tentative and rare in the issues of grief. Most grievers live their way into answers.

What are the goals of a mutual-help grief group?

- ☐ *Helps grieving people discover they are not alone.* Some grievers feel isolated from family and friends who have "moved on." Some feel alone because family members and friends will not talk about the loss.
- ☐ *Teaches grieving people that other grievers can be trusted.* Grievers are like seasoned travelers, so they share tips from the path. There will be times when someone will share in such a way that you will conclude, "So I am not crazy, after all!" or "I am not the only one experiencing this!"
- ☐ *Teaches grieving people that the story of another griever may have raw resources for their healing.* Some griever in the group has raw resources that will make a difference in your grief and in your life.
- ☐ *Encourages grieving people to honestly express their feelings.*
- ☐ *Helps people healthily share emotions and stories.* All grievers have stories, emotions, and questions that have been repressed, discounted, and shamed: "You shouldn't feel that way."
- ☐ *Encourages grievers to pay attention to grief.* If you don't pay attention to grief, it will get your attention in ways that will be uncomfortable.
- ☐ *Helps grieving individuals recognize and process their feelings.* Feelings are not the problem. It's what you do with your feelings that can complicate and lighten your grief. You may have nega-

tive feelings toward God, doctors and medical personnel, persons or circumstances believed responsible for the death, even the person who died, or persons who have failed to offer support or who have stopped offering support.

- ☐ *Helps grieving persons find "companions" for the grief path.* Grievers need sidekicks to be with them on the trail. You are not called to be the Lone Ranger.

(These guidelines are based on the book by Harold Ivan Smith, *Death and Grief: Healing Through Group Support* [Minneapolis: Augsburg, 1995]).

What if someone starts crying or breaks down?

Tears are to stories what periods are to sentences. Almost every great person of faith in the Bible cried. It is no accident that the shortest verse in the Bible is "Jesus wept" (when His friend Lazarus died, John 11:35). This group may be one of the few places some feel comfortable crying. Don't rush to offer another group member a tissue. Too many times when someone hands a griever a tissue, he or she stops crying. A tissue can signal our discomfort. On the other hand, some people will not cry. That does not mean they are not grieving. We want this mutual-help group to be a safe place to cry.

Sometimes the only appropriate punctuation for a story is tears.

Why do I need a group?

Possibly because this culture—and many of its institutions—are not comfortable with grief. In a "grief-lite" culture, it might feel as if there is a "timer" on your grief. We are impatient to "complete" our grief or control it.

Mourning is a privilege

Take a moment to reflect on these words by Patrick Farmer: "Mourning is not an illness, is not a weakness, is not a self indulgence or reprehensible bad habit, but rather mourning is an essential psychological process that must be recognized and facilitated" (Patrick J. Farmer, "Bereavement Counseling," *Journal of Pastoral Counseling* 15, No. 2 [1980], 32).

What can I expect of other grievers in this mutual-help grief group?

- ☐ *Attentiveness.* Reflectively listening to another's story or comments is as important as sharing one's own story and comments. The goal is for "thoughtful and respectful listening." Sometimes we come to appreciate a person's words later in the week or long after the group has ended.
- ☐ *Participation.* Some grievers are group shy. They worry about getting their words and thoughts out in a logical format. In a mutual-help grief group, you will be encouraged: "Just tell us the way you are thinking it, and we will sort it out together." In short, you will be asked to be a responsible participant. All members contribute "firewood" to keep the fire going and glowing.
- ☐ *Eye contact.* You will be encouraged to look at each other as you tell and listen to stories. Sometimes a griever can find great encouragement in a smile, in a nod that conveys, "I know what you mean!" or "Yes, I've experienced that too."
- ☐ *Confidentiality.* While this is not a 12-step group, confidentiality will be appreciated and expected. "What is said here, stays *here."*

What will I be asked to do through participating in a mutual-help grief gathering?

You will only be asked to be yourself and to give your grief its voice. Wonderful things happen when people share their grief.

4
NAMING RITUALS*

▶ Many grievers have difficulty remembering the funeral rituals for their loved ones. Some were numb; others took a "just get me through this" attitude. So this ritual of closure, called "the naming," offers a chance to create a memory.

The pastor or leader can conduct this ritual in one of several ways. It can be used to close a mutual-help group. Some may wish to use it with families in an informal setting. Others may conduct a once-a-year service in the chapel or sanctuary.

I suggest using a table with some type of cloth. In the center have one burning candle. In a semicircle arrange one unlit candle for each member of the group. At the designated point, as the name of the loved one is called, the individual will step to the table and light his or her candle. Then the individual turns and tells the group one characteristic of the loved one he or she wants the group to remember.

Allow them to take the candle as a symbol of the group experiences.

Use the following as a guideline in designing your naming ritual.

---

*Printable and adaptable versions of these naming rituals are included on *The Grief Care Kit* CD.

[Date]

[Name of Church]

The Naming

[Name(s) of facilitator(s) of mutual-help group]
We have gathered in this moment and in this place to name,
to remember, to honor, to give gratitude to God
for the capacity to love
and for the capacity to grieve.

Please recite-read the words in bold in unison.

In the hallways of my memories and the canyons of my heart,
[Name], I will always remember you!
In the soft snows of winter and the hot spells of summer,
[Name], I will always remember you!
In the dawn of spring and the dawn of fall,
[Name], I will always remember you!
On birthdays, anniversaries, and ordinary days,
[Name], I will always remember you!
When I am lonely and tempted to be bitter,
[Name], I will always remember you!
When I am disheartened and confused,
[Name], I will always remember you!
When good news is too good to keep to myself,
[Name], I will always remember you!
In the candlelight of Christmas and in the dawning of Easter,
[Name], I will always remember you!

Scripture

"I am the resurrection and the life. He who believes in me will live, even though he dies; and whoever lives and believes in me will never die. Do you believe this?" (John 11:25-26).

"Do not let your hearts be troubled. Trust in God; trust also in me. In my Father's house are many rooms; if it were not so, I would have told you. I am going there to prepare a place for you. And if I go and prepare a place for you, I will come back and take you to be with me that you also may be where I am" (14:1-3).

A Prayer

God, You endowed me with the ability to love, to remember, to honor, and to miss [say aloud your loved one's first name].
Open my grief-ravaged heart and grief-filmed eyes to see more clearly, to remember more honestly, and to love in new ways.
Give me wisdom to grieve thoroughly.
Give me courage to give grief a voice.
Give me strength to trust You when I cannot understand.
Keep me from becoming bitter and cynical.
Strengthen my belief in heaven and a joyous reunion with those who have gone ahead. Amen.

A Reflection

"As we pass through our earthly life, we're **giving,** taking, **experiencing,** sharing, **loving,** and struggling. We are here on a visa, **for this is not our permanent home.** Finding a quiet place can remind us that after we die, **we will come home to where our passport is valid.**"

--Malcolm Boyd[1]

The Griever's Petition for Healing Grace

LEADER: For those times I said too much
GRIEVERS: Lord, bring me healing.
LEADER: For those times I said too little
GRIEVERS: Lord, bring me healing.
LEADER: For those times I didn't encourage
GRIEVERS: Lord, bring me healing.
LEADER: For those times I discouraged a dream
GRIEVERS: Lord, bring me healing.
LEADER: For those little resentments I chose to cling to
GRIEVERS: Lord, bring me healing.
LEADER: For those times I did not fully appreciate love
GRIEVERS: Lord, bring me healing.

The Calling of the Names

As the name(s) of your loved one(s) is (are) read, come forward and light a candle. Then share one characteristic of your loved one with the group.

Lynne Harper, wife	**remembered by John Harper**
Frank A. Harris, grandfather	**remembered by Debbie Harris**
Millie Harris, grandmother	**remembered by Kristen Smith**
Pam Huddleston, sister	**remembered by Mavis Huddleston**
Wanda Taylor, daughter	**remembered by David Huddleston**

Lars Hanson, husband — **remembered by Anna Hanson**
Peter Tong, friend — **remembered by Jane Anderson**

The Closing Prayer

God, You have promised to be close to the brokenhearted. Abraham wept at the death of his beloved wife, Sarah. David wept at the death of his sons. Jesus wept at the death of His friend Lazarus. We thank You for these courageous grievers who have been part of this mutual-help grief group. They have acknowledged their griefs. They have carried one another's burdens. Bless them as they walk forward on this path called grief. Give them strength sufficient for the demands of these days. Bring us safely to Your heavenly kingdom where there will be no more death or mourning or crying or pain. Amen.

[Turn to someone and say] **May their memory to us be a blessing**!

Optional Blessing

May God who walked the dusty road
to Emmaus with grievers
bend low to you
these grief-filled days.
May your path frequently lead
to that oasis called courage.
May your eyesight rest on a closer horizon
colored with hope.
May you never lose hope
in God's incredible mercy,
new every morning,
sufficient for the demands
of any day.

The Naming at Christmas

The holidays can be devastating for grievers—not just the first Christmas, because the mourner may be numb. Particular Christmases can be difficult. Christmas is such a "family-oriented" holiday. What is needed is a safe place to honor the grief while everyone else seems to be "making merry."

This offers your church an incredible opportunity to reach out to grievers in the community. This special service can, in the words of the hymn, offer "strength for today and bright hope for tomorrow."

Some churches elect to have the service on a Sunday afternoon in December. You may decide to ask a local funeral home to cosponsor the event with you. It is important to announce and publicize the event well in advance because of the hectic schedules of the holidays.

It is helpful to ask people to sign up in advance. But plan for more participants at the door.

Focus the service around the Communion table. Place a large Nativity scene on the table. At an appropriate moment in the service, grievers will be asked to come forward and light a votive candle and place it at the manger.

Or you may want to focus on a manger with straw. Pass out cards and ask grievers to write the names of their loved ones on the cards and place them in the manger.

Because candles are such a part of the holiday season, consider using candles.

Some congregations prepare gift ornaments. Take a simple gold ornament (or red or green), tie a black ribbon on it to symbolize the death, and write the name of the deceased on the ornament if you have someone with calligraphy skills. The participants take the ornaments with them.

A remembrance tree can also be important. Decorate a Christmas tree with white lights, and place it in a prominent place in your church. Then prepare paper ornaments (perhaps in the shape of angels or snowflakes) and have participants sign the names of the deceased with a gold pen. Later in the service of remembrance they will hang them on the tree.

The goal is to acknowledge the loss in the holiday season rather than pretend the loss did not occur.

Many churches have found that having punch/coffee and holiday cookies before and/or after the event can make people feel more comfortable.

Realize, too, that it may take a couple of years for this remembrance tradition to take hold in a church or a community.

Naming the Name

There are two options for naming the name of the loved one. First, on a registration card, you may have the participants print the name. Then at the appropriate time in the service, as the name is read, one or more individuals come forward to light a candle and place at the manger.

Or have participants come to a microphone (especially if it is a large group), and have them say the name and relationship.

Ask members of your congregation to come with a griever or to invite someone they know who is grieving this holiday season. Music is an important element in this service.

Additional resources may be found in the book by Harold Ivan Smith, ***Journaling Your Decembered Grief*** (Kansas City: Beacon Hill Press of Kansas City, 2001).

[Date]

[Name of Church]

A Time to Remember

Please recite-read in unison the words in bold.

Music

Welcoming [Offer words of welcome, then say]

We have gathered in the middle of this busy holiday season
to name,
to remember, to honor, to give gratitude to God
for the capacity to love
and for the capacity to grieve.
In one sense, we are not here because someone died,
we are here because someone *lived!*
And we are here because the Babe of Bethlehem
grew up to conquer death and the grave.
We are here because the One who had lain in a manger promises:
"Blessed are those who mourn,
for they will be comforted."

Music

Prayer

Scripture Reading--The Christmas Story (Luke 2:1-15)

The Recognition of Loss

Along the hallways of my memories and in the canyons of my heart,
[Name], I will always remember you!
In the soft snows of winter and the glow of Christmas,
[Name], I will always remember you!
In the stirring beauty of the Christmas music,
[Name], I will always remember you!
I will remember the gifts you gave; I will remember the gift of love.
[Name], I will always remember you!
When I am lonely and tempted to be cynical,

[Name], I will always remember you!
When I am tempted to mumble or scream, "Christmas? Bah, humbug!"
[Name], I will always remember you!
In the candlelight and scents of Christmas,
[Name], I will always remember you!

A Prayer

God, You endowed us with the ability to love, to remember, to honor, and to miss [say aloud your loved one's first name].
Open our grief-ravaged heart and grief-filmed eyes to see more clearly, **to remember more honestly,** and to love in new ways.
Give us wisdom **to grieve thoroughly.**
Give us courage to give grief a voice in this holiday season.
Give us strength to trust You when we cannot understand.
Strengthen our belief in heaven **where every day is Christmas! Amen.**

A Reflection

"Despite everything going on in the world, God notices your grief. Your grief has not and will not escape God's attention. He will work to reach out to you in this season."

--Harold Ivan Smith[2]

[Pastor can expand on this thought.]

Optional Griever's Petition for Healing Grace

LEADER: For those times I said too much
GRIEVERS: Lord, bring me healing.
LEADER: For those times I said too little
GRIEVERS: Lord, bring me healing.
LEADER: For those times I took so much for granted
GRIEVERS: Lord, bring me healing.
LEADER: For those times I discouraged a dream
GRIEVERS: Lord, bring me healing.
LEADER: For those little resentments I chose to cling to
GRIEVERS: Lord, bring me healing.
LEADER: For those times I did not fully appreciate love
GRIEVERS: Lord, bring me healing.

The Calling of the Names

As the name(s) of your loved one(s) is (are) read, come forward and light a candle.

[Optional: Come forward and say your loved one's name and light a candle. Then return to your seat. If you wish, share one characteristic of your loved one with the group.]

Music

"Silent Night!" [Congregation or a solo]

The Closing Prayer

God, You have promised to be close to the brokenhearted. You heard the cries of the mothers weeping at the death of their babies after Herod's outrageous brutality. You do not ask us to deny or hide our grief. Rather, You acknowledged the reality of mourning when You said, "Blessed are those who mourn." Give us in this holiday season the courage to believe Your promise: "For they will be comforted" (Matt. 5:4). We thank You for these courageous grievers who have been part of this service of remembrance. These candles remind us that You are the Light of the World. Give us all strength sufficient for the demands of these holidays. Bring us safely to Your heavenly kingdom where there will be no more death or mourning or crying or pain. Amen.

[Turn to someone and say] **May their memory to us be a blessing!**

Optional Blessing

May God who walked the dusty road
    to Emmaus with grievers
    bend low to you
    these grief-filled days.

Thank you for honoring the life of your loved one with us in this special service of remembrance. It is our prayer that you will continue to celebrate the gift of your loved one's life, joys shared, and cherished memories throughout this Christmas season.

The Naming for Mother's Day

Name the two busiest days of the year for florists and that would be Valentine's Day and Mother's Day. Mother's Day is celebrated because of the determined persistence of one grieving daughter Anna Jarvis. Anna had often heard her mother, Anna R. Jarvis, remark that she wished someone would start a special day to honor mothers. Mrs. Jarvis's death in 1905 galvanized her daughter, Anna M., into action. She organized a four-hour service in Grafton, West Virginia, saluting mothers on May 10, 1908, because it was the Sunday closest to the anniversary of her mother's death (May 9). Anna initiated the tradition of red and white carnations by passing out carnations (red if a mother was living, white if deceased) because the carnation had been her mother's favorite flower.

Anna identified four purposes for the first celebration: (1) to honor mothers, (2) to bring families together, (3) to make better children, and (4) to brighten the lives of good mothers. Over the next years, Anna worked tirelessly writing thousands of letters to influential persons to enlist their support. The encouragement of Philadelphia department store owner John Wanamaker—who recognized the sales potential for such a day—gave the effort national visibility and recognition.

Initially, governors proclaimed state "mother's days." In 1914 a group of devoted sons introduced legislation in Congress to establish the second Sunday in May as a national Mother's Day. The bill was passed without a single negative vote (imagine running for reelection explaining why you voted against mothers!). President Woodrow Wilson immediately signed the legislation.

One grieving daughter gave the country a great gift. Never underestimate the ability of a griever to make a difference. Great ideas begin with courageous grievers who say, "Could we?"

Overview

Mother's Day can be devastating for individuals grieving the deaths of their mothers and for mothers grieving the deaths of children; for many, it is a bittersweet day. The first Mother's Day, the son or daughter may be numb. Grievers need a safe place to honor the grief while everyone else seems to be honoring their mothers with gifts, flowers, and brunches.

You have an incredible opportunity to reach out to grievers in your church and in the community. This special service can, in the words of the hymn, offer "strength for today and bright hope for tomorrow."

Some churches schedule the service midafternoon on Mother's Day so as not to interfere with family gatherings. It is important to announce the event well in advance. You may enlist a local funeral home to cosponsor the event with you.

It may be helpful to ask people to sign up in advance. But plan for some to just show up.

One idea for a theme is to use a large grapevine wreath. At the registration table have long strips of colorful ribbon or pastel-colored ribbon. Ask participants to write their mothers' names on the ribbons. During the "naming of the names," ask grievers to come forward and say their mothers' names and tie the ribbons to the wreath. Slowly, the wreath that will seem stark will take color.

Consider offering a carnation to each participant.

The goal is to acknowledge the loss on this Mother's Day rather than pretend the loss did not occur.

Providing light refreshments before and/or after the event can make people feel more comfortable, particularly visitors to your church.

Realize, too, that it may take a couple of years for this remembrance tradition to take hold in a church or a community.

There are two options for naming the name of the loved one. First, on registration cards, you may have participants print their mothers' names. (Make certain that whoever reads the names can pronounce them.) Then at the appropriate time in the service, each name is read aloud and the individual or individuals come forward to tie a ribbon on the wreath.

Or have participants come to a microphone (especially if a large group), and have them say the names of their mothers and one characteristic they would like remembered about each one of them.

Ask members of your congregation to attend with a griever or to invite someone they know who is grieving this holiday season. Music is an important element in this service.

What follows is open to modification to meet the needs of the group. The facilitator may lead the ritual. A pastor or member of the pastoral staff of the church may be invited to provide leadership or offer brief words.

You may also want to include a reading of Robert Munsch's delightful book Love You Forever (Scarborough, Ont.: Firefly Books, 1986).

Some groups may use candles. Use the Communion table with some type of cloth. In the center have one burning candle. At the designated point, as the name of the loved one is called, the individual(s) will step to the table and light a candle to place on the Communion table. Then ask the individual(s) to turn and tell the group one characteristic of the mother being remembered.

Allow them to take the candle as a symbol of the remembrance service.

It is not necessary to use all the material provided. Use this as a resource to create your service of remembrance.

[Date]

[Name of Church]

The Honoring of Mothers

[Name(s) of facilitator of mutual-help group]

"But at any age, the loss of a mother is a special bereavement. To be cut off from the one who bore us, nourished us, and taught us the first and deepest lessons of life leaves us lonely in a way no other deprivation can."

--F. J. Bowman to Harry S. Truman[3]

"People must be given the opportunity to hurt out loud."

--Lady Bird Johnson[4]

We have gathered in this moment and in this place to name,
to remember, to honor, to give gratitude to God
for mothers who have died.

Please recite-read the words in bold in unison.

Prayer

Blessed are those who mourn,
for they shall be comforted.
Lord, I have heard this beatitude
since my mother taught it to me.
Now, in her absence,
help me to discover its truth.

Reading

How can it be Mother's Day? You are not here.
I feel like a motherless child.
You are not here to receive my card.
I feel like a motherless child.
You are not here to receive my gift.
I feel like a motherless child.
You are not here to receive my hug.
I feel like a motherless child.
You are not here to hug me back.
I feel like a motherless child.
Yet you are here!

Along the corridors of my memory
you bake and wash,
bathe and touch,
scold and question,
comfort and soothe.
This Mother's Day I will wander through my memories
remembering how you mothered me.

Music

A Prayer

Lord, for that for which I am grateful;
for that which, in time, I hope to be grateful;
for that which I am not yet ready to be grateful,
enable me to find and to create gratitude
to honor
this remarkable woman I have called Mom.

Scripture

"Honor your father and your mother, so that you may live long in the land the LORD your God is giving you" (Exod. 20:12).

"Who can find a virtuous woman? . . ." (Prov. 31:10-31, KJV).

Reading 1

"No matter how we struggle to be wholly separate, no matter how far away we plant ourselves, we are destined to exist in relation to our mothers, to the very source of our lives. Our achievements are their achievements. Our failures are their failures. Our dreams are only variations of those our mothers dreamed for us. We reject their expectations, or strive to live up to them, but we live our lives forever in the shadows of theirs."

--Joie Davidow[5]

Silence [Or Prov. 31:14-17]

Reading 2

"There was no longer anyone who would ever again claim me as their child. No longer was anyone living who had been present at my birth, who had witnessed my first steps, heard my first words, walked me to my first day of school, or paced the floor, nervously, the first time I borrowed the family car. No one knew the details of my life and my family's history. I was no longer anyone's child."

--Alexander Levy[6]

Silence [Or Prov. 31:18-22]

Reading 3

"Moms are not supposed to die. Moms are like bronze statues, around for a lifetime. Moms are like family heirlooms; they get handed down from generation to generation. Moms don't die. We still had too much to say to each other, too much to do together, too much more ahead. What are we supposed to do without you, Mom?"

--Michelle Windmueller[7]

Silence [Or Prov. 31:23-27]

Reading 4

"My mother and I shared so many things: lollipops, lace hankies, hair barrettes, girlish secrets, and a passion for chocolate-covered cherries. We sang camp songs, and she taught me how to make 's'mores.' She showed me how to make a great meatloaf and even lump-free gravy. In fact, my mom taught me everything--except how to live without her."

--Darcie Sims[8]

Silence [Or Prov. 31:28-31]

The Griever's Petition for Healing Grace

LEADER: For those times I said too much
GRIEVERS: Lord, bring me healing.
LEADER: For those times I said too little
GRIEVERS: Lord, bring me healing.
LEADER: For those times I didn't respect my mother
GRIEVERS: Lord, bring me healing.
LEADER: For those times I broke her heart
GRIEVERS: Lord, bring me healing.
LEADER: For those little resentments and annoyances I have chosen to cling to
GRIEVERS: Lord, bring me healing.
LEADER: For those times I did not fully appreciate her love
GRIEVERS: Lord, bring me healing.
LEADER: Lord, for giving me this particular mother
GRIEVERS: Lord, thank You.

The Calling of the Names

As the name(s) of your loved one(s) is (are) read, come forward and light a candle. Then share one characteristic of your loved one with the group.

Reflection

During these grief-filled days
I hold tightly to one nonnegotiable belief:
I will see my mother again.
While I do not understand all the details of the promise,
I do believe in the One who made the promise.
In those moments when I feel
ambushed by grief, again,
I am comforted by Jesus' promise
to "go away and prepare a place."
Jesus can be taken seriously.

The Closing Prayer

Lord,
use the words, stories, and memories of others
who have lost mothers
to prompt my words, stories, and memories.
Give me courage to own my loss
and to grieve well. Amen.

[Turn to someone and say] **May their memory to us be a blessing!**

NOTES

1. Malcolm Boyd, *Go Gentle into the Night* (Columbus, Miss.: Genesis Press, 1998), 70.

2. Harold Ivan Smith, *Journaling Your Decembered Grief* (Kansas City: Beacon Hill Press of Kansas City, 2001), 34.

3. F. J. Bowman to Harry S. Truman, 31 July 1947, Truman Presidential Library.

4. Jan Jarboe Russell, *Lady Bird: A Biography of Mrs. Johnson* (New York: Scribner, 1999), 53.

5. Joie Davidow and Esmerald Santiago, eds., introduction to *Las Mamis: Famous Latino Authors Remember Their Mothers* (New York: Knopf, 2000), ix.

6. Alexander Levy, *The Orphaned Child: Understanding and Coping with Grief and Change After the Death of Our Parents* (Cambridge, Mass.: Perseus Publishing, 1999), 46.

7. Michelle Windmueller, personal correspondence, 24 April 2002.

8. Darcie Sims, quoted in Richard Gilbert, *Finding Your Way After Your Parent Dies* (Notre Dame, Ind.: Ave Maria Press, 1999), 11.

5
QUOTES

▶ Words—sometimes when we do not have words, we borrow them. In this chapter you will find words that many grievers have found helpful. I have used these in my groups for years. I call them "refrigerator quotes." I ask participants to put a quote on the refrigerator so that others can see it; who knows, it might spark conversation. Moreover, that quote will be a reminder to the griever.

I have found these quotes helpful to send with a letter to a grieving individual. You can find these quotes and several more on the CD. Look through them, and find one that is appropriate as a supplement to your words. You can then paste it in your letter or print a separate copy.

These quotes can also be used to jump-start discussions in the mutual-help group or in counseling. Ask participants to read the quotation twice. Then ask them to take a moment to reflect on the quote. Follow this up by asking, "Did any word or phrase 'leap out' at you when you read the quotation?"

Finally, these quotes will be useful as you prepare funeral or memorial service sermons. I would suggest that you begin gathering your own quote collection. Keeping them with this kit might make them more accessible when you need them.

Quote 1

God
does not waste
an ounce of our pain
or a drop of our tears;
suffering doesn't come
our way for no reason,
and He seems
especially efficient
at using what we endure
to mold our character.
If we are malleable,
He takes our bumps
and bruises and
shapes them into
something beautiful.

—Frank Peretti, *The Wounded Spirit* (Nashville: Word, 2001), 183

Quote 2

WE are changed by those we love who have left us, because we were formed by them while they were here.

WHEN someone dies or leaves, we have to revisit in new ways the places they inhabited in our hearts. It is not so much that we take part of them into us as that, in their absence, we discover or cultivate a part of us we did not know was there. This does not compensate for their loss. The loss is still loss, but our creative healing becomes part of their legacy to us.

—Susan Ford Wiltshire
Athena's Disguises (Louisville, Ky.: Westminster, 1999), 135

Quote 3

People must be given the opportunity to hurt out loud.

—Lady Bird Johnson
Quoted in Jan Jarboe Russell
Lady Bird: A Biography of Mrs. Johnson
(New York: Scribner, 1999), 53

Quote 4

God, be in my head . . . and in my understanding.

God, be in my eyes . . . and in my looking.

God, be in my mouth . . . and in my speaking.

God, be in my heart . . . and in my thinking.

God, be in my grieving . . . and in my healing.

—Adapted from *Book of Hours* (1514)

Quote 5

Remembering the person

I have loved allows me to slowly heal.

Healing does not mean I will forget.

Actually, it means **I will** remember.

Gently, **I will** move forward,

never forgetting my past.

—Alan D. Wolfelt
Creating Meaningful Ceremonies
(Fort Collins, Colo.: Companion Press, 1997), 47

Quote 6

Right now, you may feel like the scattered pieces of a broken puzzle. Honor that feeling, but also take comfort in knowing that the pieces of a puzzle can be reshuffled, rearranged, and pieced together to form a new picture. As you learn to create a new reality for yourself, temper your expectations with compassion and gentleness.

Slowly, gently, I have begun to focus on my loved one's life—not the death—and that has made all the difference.

—Darcie Sims, bereaved parent
Getting Through the Holidays, CareNotes
(St. Meinrad, Ind.: Abbey Press, 1996), 7

Quote 7

YOU MAY HAVE HEARD
indeed you may believe
that your grief's journey end will come
when you resolve, or recover from,
your grief.

But you may also be coming to understand
one of the fundamental truths of grief:
Your journey will never end.

People do not "get over" grief.
My personal and professional experience
tells me that a total return to "normalcy"
after the death of someone loved
is not possible;
we are forever changed
by the experience of grief.

—Alan D. Wolfelt
The Journey Through Grief
(Fort Collins, Colo.: Compassion Books, 1997), 135

Quote 8

When is this grief going to be over?
Asking when mourning is finished is a little
like asking how high is up?
One benchmark of a completed grief
reaction is when
the person is able to think of the deceased
without pain.
There is always a sense of sadness when you
think
of someone that you have loved and lost,
but it is a
different kind of sadness—it lacks the
wrenching quality
it previously had.

—J. William Worden
Grief Counseling and Grief Therapy:
A Handbook for the Mental Health Practitioner, 2d. ed.
(New York: Springer, 1991), 18

Quote 9

Death

is not a period that ends the great sentences

of life, but a comma that punctuates it to more lofty

significance . . .

God

is able . . . to transform dark and desolate valleys

into sunlit paths of inner peace.

—Martin Luther King Jr.
Quoted in Gerald K. Zelizer, "King, Rabbi Expose What New Age Religion Lacks,"
USA Today, 18 January 1998, 13A

Quote 10

Go **confidently**

into the direction of **your** future.

God is already there.

—Harold Ivan Smith

Quote 11

The most useful lesson
that a griever can learn about the holidays
is this:
Sometimes
there's no way around,
no way under,
no way over.
Sometimes
the only way is
through!

—Harold Ivan Smith

Quote 12

I have come to believe
in a future Christmas
when all God's children
will be home.

The God
who gave The Gift
on that first Christmas
promises an incredible agenda:

"He will
wipe every tear
from their eyes.
There will be no more
death or mourning
or crying or pain"
(Rev. 21:4).

AND
the celebration will never stop.

—Harold Ivan Smith
Journaling Your Decembered Grief
(Kansas City: Beacon Hill Press of Kansas City, 2001), 78

Quote 13

"Oh, but you have lots of friends . . ."
"Left" is the word they do not say.
That's what people told me when I mentioned
my friend's death.
Although I am blessed
with a rich bounty of friends,
I am still diminished
by the loss of any one of them.
Because with their passing
a chunk of my past and future ends.
Who will be there to ask:
"Do you remember the time?"

No one, these days,
has friends to spare.
It would be like saying
to the curator of an art museum
after a masterpiece had been stolen,
"Oh, but you still have lots of paintings . . ."
Perhaps.
"But I had only one that hung there."

Give your grief its voice.
Pay attention to your memories.
And count the ways you have been blessed
by having such a friend.

—Harold Ivan Smith
Friendgrief: An Absence Called Presence
(Amityville: N.Y.: Baywood, 2001), iv

Quote 14

We walk innocently
into our griefs,
and they carry us
wherever we have to go
in order to learn,
to find meaning,
to reach some kind of peaceful
acceptance.
We cannot control them;
we ride them like a runaway horse.
Our job is to stay on
until the horse calms down and
we are allowed to walk awhile,
to retake the reins.

—Christina Baldwin
One to One: Self Understanding Through Journal Writing
(New York: M. Evans and Company, 1991), 155-56

Quote 15

In a society
which is much more inclined
to help you hide your pain
rather than to grow through it,
it is necessary to make a very
conscious effort to mourn.

—Henri Nouwen
In Memoriam (Notre Dame, Ind.: Ave Maria Press, 1980), 158

Quote 16

GRIEVING

is a journey that teaches us how to love in a new way now that our loved one is no longer with us. This journey from loving in presence to loving in absence is possible because the lives of those who have loved remain real in the lives of those of us who knew and loved them. The times we spent together are not erased from history.

We retain our unique acquaintance with those we love.

We still hold memories that we can review privately or share with one another.

We still feel the imprints of their lives on us where we hold their practical, soulful, and spiritual legacies.

CONSCIOUSLY REMEMBERING

those who have died is the key that opens our hearts, that allows us to love them in new ways.

AS WE REMEMBER

what we love about those who have died, we welcome them back into our lives even though we are apart. We begin to learn how to love them in new ways. In memory we can cherish them. We can carry them with us into the future.

—Thomas Attig
The Heart of Grief (New York: Oxford Press, 2000), 27

Quote 17

You close on a house.
You don't close on a death.

—Peggy Broxterman, who lost a son
in the Oklahoma City bombing, scoffing
at the idea that the execution of Timothy McVeigh
will bring "closure," "Perspective," *Newsweek,* May 7, 2001, 21

6
HYMN TEXTS

▶ Never underestimate the power of a hymn recalled, whether sung or read, to be a source of encouragement to grievers. There are several ways to use these hymn texts and the CD.*

1. During your preparation for a funeral or memorial service, or for a group session, listening to a hymn may offer you a particular insight. These seven hymns were carefully selected for the project because of the hope offered in their lyrics.
2. In counseling, you may ask a counselee to sit and listen to a hymn or to read the lyrics. Ask, "What comes to your mind and heart when you hear these words or this tune?"
3. Incorporate the lyrics into the body of a letter. Paul wrote the Ephesian Christians, "Speak to one another with psalms, hymns and spiritual songs" (Eph. 5:19). We often forget that the Book of Psalms has been a Jewish hymnbook that has comforted generations of grievers in their darkest moments.
4. In the mutual-help group you might play one of the hymns as the group gathers. It will set a mood for the helpful work that will take place in the group. You might ask participants to follow the words. Or you might even ask them to sing along. Paul also counseled the Ephesians, "Sing and make music in your heart to the Lord" (v. 19). Some grievers will not be able to sing; but they can "hear" the hymn text "in [their] heart."

---

*See page 5 for instructions about accessing audio and text files on *The Grief Care Kit* CD. Printable versions of the hymn texts are included on the CD.

Hymn Text 1

Day by Day

(1)

Day by day, and with each passing moment,
Strength I find to meet my trials here.
Trusting in my Father's wise bestowment,
I've no cause for worry or for fear.
He whose heart is kind beyond all measure
Gives unto each day what He deems best,
Lovingly its part of pain and pleasure,
Mingling toil with peace and rest.

(2)

Ev'ry day the Lord Himself is near me,
With a special mercy for each hour.
All my cares He fain would bear and cheer me,
He whose name is Counselor and Pow'r.
The protection of His child and treasure
Is a charge that on Himself He laid.
"As thy days, thy strength shall be in measure,"
This the pledge to me He made.

(3)

Help me then, in ev'ry tribulation,
So to trust Thy promises, O Lord,
That I lose not faith's sweet consolation,
Offered me within Thy holy Word.
Help me, Lord, when toil and trouble meeting,
E'er to take, as from a Father's hand,
One by one, the days, the moments fleeting,
Till I reach the promise land.

—Caroline V. Sandell-Berg (*Sing to the Lord,* 105)

Hymn Text 2

Precious Memories

(1)

As I travel down life's pathway,
Know not what the years may hold.
As I ponder, hopes grow fonder,
Precious memories flood my soul.

(Refrain)

Precious memories, how they linger,
How they ever flood my soul.
In the stillness of the midnight,
Precious sacred scenes unfold.

(2)

Precious father, loving mother,
Glide across the lonely years.
And old home scenes from my childhood
In fond memory appears.

—Traditional folk song, words by J. B. F. Wright

Hymn Text 3

Does Jesus Care?

(1)

Does Jesus care when my heart is pained
Too deeply for mirth and song,
As the burdens press, And the cares distress,
And the way goes weary and long?

(Refrain)

O yes, He cares; I know He cares!
His heart is touched with my grief.
When the days are weary, The long nights dreary,
I know my Savior cares.

(2)

Does Jesus care when my way is dark
With a nameless dread and fear?
As the daylight fades Into deep night shades,
Does He care enough to be near?

(3)

Does Jesus care when I've said good-bye
To the dearest on earth to me,
And my sad heart aches Till it nearly breaks?
Is it aught to Him? Does He see?

—Frank E. Graeff (*Sing to the Lord,* 574)

Hymn Text 4

What a Friend We Have in Jesus

(1)

What a Friend we have in Jesus,
All our sins and griefs to bear!
What a privilege to carry
Ev'rything to God in prayer!
O what peace we often forfeit,
O what needless pain we bear,
All because we do not carry
Ev'rything to God in prayer!

(2)

Have we trials and temptations?
Is there trouble anywhere?
We should never be discouraged;
Take it to the Lord in prayer.
Can we find a friend so faithful
Who will all our sorrows share?
Jesus knows our ev'ry weakness;
Take it to the Lord in prayer.

(3)

Are we weak and heavy-laden,
Cumbered with a load of care?
Precious Savior, still our Refuge!
Take it to the Lord in prayer.
Do thy friends despise, forsake thee?
Take it to the Lord in prayer.
In His arms He'll take and shield thee;
Thou wilt find a solace there.

—Joseph M. Scriven (*Sing to the Lord,* 625)

Hymn Text 5

He Keeps Me Singing

(1)

There's within my heart a melody.
Jesus whispers sweet and low:
"Fear not, I am with thee; peace, be still,"
In all of life's ebb and flow.

(Refrain)

Jesus, Jesus, Jesus—
Sweetest name I know,
Fills my ev'ry longing,
Keeps me singing as I go.

(2)

Tho' sometimes He leads thro' waters deep,
Trials fall across the way,
Tho' sometimes the path seems rough and steep,
See His footprints all the way.

—Luther B. Bridgers (*Sing to the Lord*, 349)

Hymn Text 6

It Is Well with My Soul

(1)

When peace like a river attendeth my way,
When sorrows like sea billows roll,
Whatever my lot, Thou hast taught me to say,
"It is well, it is well with my soul."

(Refrain)

It is well with my soul.
It is well, it is well with my soul.

(2)

Tho' Satan should buffet, tho' trials should come,
Let this blest assurance control,
That Christ hath regarded my helpless estate,
And hath shed His own blood for my soul.

(3)

And, Lord, haste the day when the faith shall be sight,
The clouds be rolled back as a scroll,
The trump shall resound and the Lord shall descend.
Even so—it is well with my soul.

—Horatio G. Spafford (*Sing to the Lord,* 554)

Hymn Text 7

He Giveth More Grace

(1)

He giveth more grace when the burdens grow greater;
He sendeth more strength when the labors increase.
To added affliction He addeth His mercy.
To multiplied trials, His multiplied peace.

(Refrain)

His love has no limit; His grace has no measure.
His pow'r has no boundary known unto men.
For out of His infinite riches in Jesus,
He giveth, and giveth, and giveth again!

(2)

When we have exhausted our store of endurance,
When our strength has failed ere the day is half done,
When we reach the end of our hoarded resources,
Our Father's full giving is only begun.

—Annie Johnson Flint* (*Sing to the Lord,* 101)

7
MUTUAL-HELP GRIEF GROUPS*

▸ Take some time to read and carefully study the following section. As you read, ask God to guide you in how such a mutual-help group could be started in your congregation. As you read, ask God to bring to mind names and faces of individuals who could benefit from such a group and names and faces of those who might help launch the group.

Then you might ask a potential leader or coleader to read through these materials. Then schedule a time to set up a meeting to discuss how a mutual-help group could be established.

This is, hopefully, not just another program but a way of providing grief care in a healthy spiritual environment—grief care that makes a difference in the lives of grievers and in the lives of a congregation.

Remember: You will learn a great deal by offering a first mutual-help group for grievers and then rereading these materials and carefully evaluating before offering a second group.

*A printable version of the contents of this chapter is included on *The Grief Care Kit* CD.

Facilitating a Mutual-Help Grief Group

"An important thing happened to me in that small gathering, and it was apparent from the very first evening when we introduced ourselves and said who we had lost and how. Telling my story and listening to those told by others in the group, I found that my experience of loss resonated with theirs in many ways, despite differences in circumstances, relationships, and so forth. We were strangers to one another. Yet I felt a strong connection with these people, as if I had found some familiar faces in a faraway place."

—Victoria Alexander[1]

Congratulations

You are about to launch an incredible adventure. As the facilitator of a mutual-help grief group, you will have opportunities to make a difference in the lives of bereaving individuals. You will have opportunities to offer "a cup of cold water," an ear, a heart in the name of Jesus.

Certainly, there will be times when you wonder, "What made me think I could lead this group?" There will be other times when you experience amazing moments of group interaction. You are not only a facilitator but also a witness to the courage of participants.

Although the gospel song "Rescue the Perishing" is often categorized as a "missions" song, it really is about the traumas that impact the human heart:

Down in the human heart, Crushed by the tempter,
Feelings lie buried that grace can restore.
Touched by a loving heart, Wakened by kindness,
Chords that are broken will vibrate once more.[2]

You will have opportunities

- To "[touch] by a loving heart," to "[waken] by kindness." God will use you to be an instrument of caring.
- To point grievers toward a grace-filled future.
- To tell grievers about Jesus and His power to redeem this loss.
- To discover that God reaches out to the grieving through care sharers, such as you.
- To be God's ambassador to grieving persons.

Vina Drennam's husband, John, a New York City fireman, died after receiving severe burns in a 1994 fire. Fortunately, Mychal Judge, a department chaplain, invested time listening and planting hope seeds. He believed that God could use her and her experience of loss. Eight years later, Vina reminisces, "After John died, Mychal opened me up to possibilities. I could have been a bitter old biddy. And no one would have criticized me for it, for we had been through so much (John had suffered in a burn unit for 40 days and nights before suffering a fatal heart attack). But he gave me a sense of obligation to sow seeds."[3]

Through your leadership and care individuals can hear empowering words: "Give your grief its voice."

Target audience

Individuals in your congregation, community, and neighborhood are grappling with the realities and complexities of grief. Some are "rookies" on the grief path. Others are veterans, although they have never experienced *this* grief. Many are numb, stunned, and confused. Some are angry after repeatedly being urged, sometimes scolded, "Get over it" or "Move on with your life." Many are disappointed that the individuals who were there for them early on in their grief experience have "moved on." In one national survey, when asked how many weeks it should take to get over a death, the majority answered two weeks. *Two weeks!*

Too many grievers grapple alone. If asked how they are doing, they respond politely, "Oh, fine. Thank you for asking." Many males find attending a mutual-help group to be a challenge. Some demand, "What good will talking do? Will it bring [Name] back?"

"No, but it will give you a setting to talk about [Name]."

The grievers who will make up your group are courageous and have chosen to be proactive rather than passive. They are choosing to grow through their grief and not just go through it. By participating in this mutual-help group they want to learn from their grief rather than *run from* it.

Grievers have three options:
to *hide* their grief,
to *discount* their grief,
to *embrace* their grief.

In this mutual-help grief group many will move from hiding or discounting their grief to embracing their grief. As a facilitator you get to be a "midwife" to the process.

The facilitator as expert or experiencer?

You are not facilitating the group as an "expert" on grief. When it comes to grief, we're all beginners.

"There are no true experts in the area of illness, dying, death, and bereavement except those who are experiencing illness, dying, and bereavement."

—Helen Wilson Harris[4]

Hopefully, you have had some firsthand experience with loss. Hopefully you are facilitating this group because you have sensed a need for such a group and have felt some sense of calling on your heart and life.

Paul's words in 2 Corinthians prod us: "Praise be to the God and Father of our Lord Jesus Christ, the Father of compassion and the God of all comfort, who comforts us in all our troubles" (1:3-4). *All our troubles?* Some grievers have difficulty believing those words. God seems absent, silent, or far on the fringes of their grief. How will those with wounded hearts and spirits receive God's comfort? Possibly through a mutual-help group—through your compassionate care.

As a facilitator you can be a conduit through which God's comfort flows.

Increasingly, Paul's words are misquoted: "Praise be to the God and Father of our Lord Jesus Christ . . . who comforts us in all our sorrows." However, there is a comma rather than a period after "troubles" (not "sorrows"): "God . . . comforts us in all our troubles, *so that* we can comfort those in any trouble with the comfort we ourselves have received from God" (emphasis added). God does not comfort us so that we can "get over" our loss and "get on with our lives." Charlotte Czillinger, whose 14-year-old daughter was murdered, concluded, "If life experiences are not used, they are wasted."[5]

Charlotte's loss has led her to work with parents of murdered children. She has learned that God comforts so that we can step into some of life's darkest moments and be God's "field reps" in the tragedy.

You perhaps have heard grievers say or have even said to grievers: "Good is going to come out of this." Some who have done time in "grief land" have acquired confidence in God's comfort to pass on to individuals whose today is their yesterday. Perhaps out of your woundedness, the grief you have grappled with, God has led you to this "so that" point of servant leadership. The promise of comfort will sound more believable coming from you.

"But isn't there someone more qualified?"

In the field of massage, many individuals are technically precise and proficient; they know how to do each of the major strokes correctly. Unfortunately, their touch is mechanical. The recipient of their massage never feels "magic" in their hands. In some cases, they were rubbed, not massaged! The massage therapist has skill but no passion. The same is true in facilitating mutual-help groups.

Yes, there may be "more qualified" individuals who could facilitate this group. They have training, perhaps psychological training, graduate degrees. They may even have experienced a significant loss themselves. But some life-qualified, credentialed individuals are not willing to embrace the grief. They are unwilling to allow themselves to be impacted by the grief of others, because it "reboots" or stirs up their own pain.

I like the story about a famous Shakespearean actor who included a recitation of the 23rd psalm in a public reading. The audience was duly impressed. Then an elderly woman stood and asked if she might recite the psalm. Although the audience heard the same words, many were moved and some wiped away tears. Later, when asked to comment on the experience, the actor explained, "Ah, I know the psalm, but she knows the Psalmist."

Some people know *about* grief. Others know grief.

The facilitator as host

A group facilitator is a host. A facilitator offers hospitality not only to grieving persons but also to their stories and the story-in-the-making. Some stories are like film in a camera; the group is a darkroom in which the pictures emerge. One of the most important gifts of a mutual-help group facilitator is presence. The caregiver is present to hear out laments and complaints, joys and befuddlements.

> **"The first task that one owes to others in the fellowship consists of listening to them."**
>
> **—Dietrich Bonhoeffer[6]**

Paraphrasing Bonhoeffer, the first task facilitators owe individuals in a mutual-help grief group is to listen to the ends of their sentences.

> **"Being invited to hear another's story is an act of trust that requires not a little courage. Ultimately it can be a moment of saving grace for the teller and the hearer."**
>
> **—Peter J. Liuzzi[7]**

Why grievers will come to this mutual-help group

- Because key people in their lives—sometimes, spouses or adult children or parents—are not listening to them
- Because key people in their lives have grown tired of hearing the griever "talk about it"
- Because some distrust mental health personnel and/or have had a negative experience in counseling
- Because other grief groups have been too therapy oriented
- Because secular groups leave out the key ingredient in grief—spirituality

Unfortunately, this faith-based mutual-help group may be the only place some grievers can freely disclose certain dimensions of their grief. This group can become a safe place for some grievers to acknowledge their anger at or disappointment in God. This group may be the spiritual space in which one participant's courage in "owning" their grief may lead another to share more deeply from their story as well.

Who knows where an act of respectful listening will lead?

Years ago a discouraged young preacher was weighing leaving the ministry in order to pursue a doctorate in philosophy; his last revival in a small town in Pennsylvania had been a disaster. Preparing for his next engagement, he was deeply troubled. Because of a scheduling error, he arrived at a retreat center a day early. He spent a long rambling conversation with the conference director, a gifted listener who "hosted" his frustration.

He left that conference renewed and walked in to preach under a large tent in Los Angeles, and the rest is history. I have often wondered what might have happened if Henrietta Mears had not been such a gracious host or had been too busy that day to "hear out" the concerns of Billy Graham. Listening was one of Miss Mears's ministry "secrets."

"I will make it easy for anyone to come to me with the deepest experiences of his [or] her inner life not by urging, but by sympathy and understanding. I will never let anyone think I am disappointed in him."[8]

Facilitators, too, "make it easy" for grievers to share from their experiences. The experience of being "listened to" influenced Graham's ministry in public and in private. In time, he learned to allow others to share their "deepest experiences" with him. In the 1950s, he was soundly criticized for spending so much time playing golf with President Dwight Eisenhower. Only in recent years has it been disclosed that they frequently talked about heaven as they played. Specifically, the president of the United States wanted assurance that he could again see his deceased mother and beloved infant son, Ikky (who had died 30 years earlier). The golf course became a "safe place" for Billy Graham to host the "still" grieving president's concerns.[9]

Miracles often happen in a circle of chairs when a mutual-help grief group meets.

The next Billy Graham may be sitting in your grief group. That Sunday afternoon Miss Mears had no idea who William Franklin Graham would become. She only knew that in that particular moment, he needed someone to listen respectfully—someone to "receive" his words, story, and confusion.

"To invite another to tell his or her story is a first mark of welcome. Such an account of the intimate moments of another's life is always a precious gift to be received with reverence and respect.

"But to fail to listen or to have an attitude that the stories of others are not worth telling—or hearing—is a serious mistake that may set the groundwork for despair and self-loathing."

—Peter J. Liuzzi[10]

Humuhumu

I am fascinated with the Hawaiian word *humuhumu,* which can mean "to fit the pieces together." Individuals will come to a mutual-help group, some rather apprehensively, fearful that no one will understand their grief experience or that no one will value what they have to share. Many will come having been bombarded with clichés. Some have been nearly "clichéd" to death! One woman vowed, "If I hear one more person quote Rom. 8:28, I am going to scream!" Some will come both expectant and hesitant.

Sadly, grief has become a medical or psychological problem to be cured and, if not cured, managed. Grief, however, is a spiritual issue. Zack Thomas expressed his hope for ministry in *Healing Touch: The Church's Forgotten Language:* "We are often broken into many pieces, but our brokenness harbors the hope that we might be reknit stronger than before."[11]

Grief
is a normal part
of the human experience to be lived,
tasted, experienced, valued, shared.

As a facilitator, your task is not to prod anyone to "get over" this loss or this latest loss (some come initially to deal with a recent loss, but other previous losses get rebooted in the process, not unlike the magician pulling colored scarves from the shirt cuff).

Your task is to be with the griever, to be *compañero* or *acompaña* (one who accompanies).

Although no one can walk your grief path for you,
someone can walk *with* you.

Someone in this mutual-help group knows something another participant needs to know. Someone further along on the grief path has a piece of wisdom that will make another's trail easier. That's why it is called a *mutual-help* group. A mutual-help group is like a potluck—everyone brings something, and no one goes away hungry. A mutual-help group is like a campfire in which everyone contributes wood.

A facilitator's task is to love, honor, and encourage the grievers God will bring to this group.

You can make a difference. This is not just a Band-Aid support to tide the griever over the demands of bereaving. This mutual-help grief group becomes a "beachhead" to reconciliation with the loss.

You do not have to know what to say

As a grief educator I have learned that sometimes there is nothing to say. Jesus demonstrated this in the initial interaction with the two grieving disciples on the road to Emmaus. His opening question to them, although He already knew the answer, was simple: "What are you discussing together as you walk along?" (Luke 24:17). His question stunned them. "They stood still, their faces downcast" until Cleopas responded, "Are you only a visitor to Jerusalem and do not know the things that have happened there in these days?" (vv. 17-18).

Jesus responded with a question, "What things?" (v. 19). Jesus was inviting these grievers to wrap words around their loss. Jesus was giving them permission to acknowledge their grief.

Jesus could have walked up to them, slapped them on the shoulders, and said, "Hey, guys, it's me! I'm back." He gave them plenty of time (in fact, they walked perhaps seven miles at a rather slow pace—a walk that took a couple of hours). He only began to counsel them after He experienced the agony in their narrative: "But we had hoped . . ." (v. 21).

Jesus is not only, in the words of the hymn, "the Great Physician" but also the great Listener. That great Listener empowers us, as facilitators, to walk the grief paths of others, not dishing out clichés, theories, or easy one, two, threes, but caring by listening.

An incident in the ministry of Corrie ten Boom illustrates this point. Because of her age, Corrie had traveling companions to make the roadwork easier and to see that she had adequate rest. One day, an aide, Pam Rosewell, curtly informed a man that Corrie was "too busy" to talk to him. Corrie challenged her: "God has sent this young man, and we will receive him."[12]

God will send you grievers. Some will be angry. Some will be numb. Some will be ignoring their own grief to concentrate on the grief of spouses, children, and grandchildren. Some will be exhausted. Some will discount their own grief. Some will challenge you. But God is "up to something" in every one of their lives.

The key qualification

The essential qualification for facilitating this group is servant listening.

- Will you listen?
- Will you listen with your eyes *and* your ears *and* heart?
- Will you listen all the way to the ends of the sentences, even those sentences that ramble?
- Will you be patient with the sentences that come in bits and pieces?
- Will you listen without rushing in and putting "words" into a griever's mouth?
- Will you listen without wanting to "rescue" individuals from their discomfort?
- Will you listen to the silences as well as the spoken words?

Honoring silence can be the healing gift of a mutual-help group.

**Many facilitators listen with their ears.
The effective facilitator listens with eyes and ears.
The sensitive facilitator listens with eyes
and ears *and* hearts.**

Your role as facilitator is something like a traffic cop—making sure that everyone goes through the intersection called "sharing" in an orderly fashion. To be sure, there may be participants who come convinced that they are experiencing the world's worst grief. "No one has experienced what I've been through!" These grievers can one-up everyone's experience. Others may be unable to initially resist the human tendency to "see you and raise you," snarling, "You think that's grief? Wait till you hear my story."

Some in your group have unbelievable grief loads or are juggling multiple griefs. You may have some whose griefs go back years, decades. A mutual-help group can provide safety for them to tell their stories. But you must be certain that the telling of those stories does not diminish the grief of others in the group who may be tempted to prorate their grief, "compared to theirs [the storytellers']."

There is no statute of limitations on grief.
All grief is major league to those carrying it.

The surprise

One surprise to some facilitating a grief group is that grievers can "bless" you. They know things that you do not know but that someday you may need to know for yourself or for a participant in a future group. You put the knowledge into escrow. Every group I have led has taught me something. When someone asks,"How do you know so much about grief?" I answer, "By hanging out with grievers."

Every individual makes a unique contribution to the group. A group will be different without that individual's participation. Remove a particular ingredient, and the recipe will not be the same. So, with groups too. If any participant does not share or come back to the second or third sessions, the group is changed.

Every grief story contains some hint of God's grace.

In the years of leading grief groups, numerous times as I have listened, I have whispered—and a few times, moaned—"O God." But more than once I have listened, reflected, then affirmed the sharer: "You are a miracle-in-progress!"

Grievers will look to you for leadership. If someone goes on and on (and they may) monopolizing the group's time, some will wonder how long you will let the person speak. If you, as a facilitator, cut short this speaker's words, others in the group will be hesitant to share their words. The mutual-help group leader must be concerned about the "flow" for the whole group in a session. Sometimes that will mean sensitively "reining in" a griever who wants the group to be focused on his or her grief rather than our griefs or who wants to keep the conversation intellectual rather than feelings oriented.

My skills as a facilitator have been shaped by the work of Rudolph Grantham, particularly his work in "lay shepherding," which suggests the existence of "redemptive" listening.

Listening is more than hearing with the ear. It is entering into the inner world of another with the purpose of being with, accepting, understanding, and helping the person understand his or her own self. It results also in helping the person arrive at a decision as to what actions are needed to resolve or live with the present life situation."

—Rudolph Grantham[13]

Jesus demonstrated redemptive listening in His Emmaus experience. In listening to a griever "try out" words for his or her loss(es), Grantham notes, "We are seeking to understand the meaning of the message to the person."[14] The goal of redemptive listening in this context is "to concentrate on the words of the speaker, not on oneself." Why? Because "often the speaker can arouse comparable feelings" in the facilitator. Thus it will be easy for the facilitator to respond—or react—to his or her own feelings rather than the speaker's.

1. The effective facilitator is a listener. Some people are incredibly gifted with listening skills. Others, through training, have become enabled to listen carefully. Listening is not some art restricted to a select few. Facilitators make time to listen thoroughly *and* ask God to give them a listening heart. Without doing violence to James

1:5, I suggest, "If any of you lacks *listening skills,* he should ask God, who gives generously to all without finding fault." Sometimes in a session, caring facilitators repeatedly have to breathe a prayer: "Lord, help me listen. *Now.*" Helen Wilson Harris contends that the "key to effective listening is to hear the story every time as though it is the first time."

"If someone needs to tell their story fifty-one times in order for it to become real and tolerable, we must not stop listening after the fiftieth hearing."

—Curtis Holland[15]

2. The effective facilitator has a reachable spirit and a teachable heart. The caring facilitator doesn't boast "I've heard it all," because until *this* griever shares his or her story, a facilitator has not heard it all at all.

3. The effective facilitator is flexible. In the years of leading groups, numerous times I have been stunned that my "design" or goals for a particular session did not happen. Under the Spirit's prompting, something else happened—something wonderful.

It's about fingertips

Look at your fingertips. No one on earth—no one—has fingerprints like yours, not even an identical twin. God went to a lot of effort to make your fingerprints distinctive and unique. Yet when it comes to facilitating a mutual-help group, some want to mimic other facilitators rather than exercise their own unique gifts. You can only be you. So facilitate as you can—not as you can't.

Let God work through you—through your unique gifts, talents, experiences, and wisdom—to facilitate this group of grieving individuals He cares deeply about.

In training facilitators, I worry about those who are overly confident: "I can do this. No sweat." As I launch each grief group I remind myself that while I have led many groups in this setting, I have never led *this* group before. "Lord, help me" is always a prayer for launching a new mutual-help grief group. Across these years God has been faithful to me. And it is not just "Lord, help me" but rather, "Lord, *keep on* helping me."

You do not have to be a "great" facilitator but a "God-led" facilitator.

"For some of us, it may be a prideful arrogance that makes us keep God at arm's length. But, for most of us, the problem is not that we can't acknowledge our limitations and inadequacies; it is rather our inability to really trust God. . . . Lacking faith and trust, we roll up our sleeves and fend for ourselves. Unfortunately, going it alone brings great stress and anxiety."

—Wilkie Au[16]

What about Kübler-Ross?

One of the dangers in helping the grieving is that people want to categorize, to place grievers in little slots. Indeed, most people can name the "five stages" of grief—denial, anger, bargaining, acceptance, and growth—widely attributed to Swiss psychiatrist Elisabeth Kübler-Ross. Many listen only long enough to decide which category a griever fits in (or *should* fit in). The assumption is that the *bereaving* proceed through grief in some orderly fashion. (The word "bereaved" illustrates our impatience; we use "bereaved"—past tense—rather than the more accurate "bereaving.") Sooner or later the griever "gets on with life," is healed or recovers. In fact, while you are reading this, somewhere grievers will be shamed for not "getting over it" as if they are failures as grievers. Others will be shamed because their continued grief is thought to be a poor reflection on God and their Christian faith, after all "he's with the Lord" or "she's in a better place."

Increasingly, grief educators and counselors are learning that grief is not completed in some neat progression of stages. Grief is not like promotion through elementary school—complete first grade in order to be promoted to second grade. That idea is too simplistic.

Everyone grieves at his or her own pace. I have come to believe, as have many of my colleagues, that the notion of grief stages not only hamstrings grief but also may complicate or sabotage a griever's pilgrimage.

Grief is not the shortest distance between two points—death and "getting over it."

Grief is like a cul-de-sac with lots of right turns, U-turns, and left turns.

"Here's what I learned about grief: It's not linear; it's not predictable. It's anything but smooth and self-contained. Someone did us all a grave injustice by implying that mourning has a distinct beginning, middle, and end."

—Hope Edelman[17]

In some instances, a griever has done all he or she can do. In the future, God will return the griever to this point, because he or she will then be better prepared to deal with it.

Let me be clear: the goal of a mutual-help grief group is *not* to help people "move on" or "get over it." The purpose is to blend this loss into the narrative of a life.

The goal of a mutual-help group is *not* to help people stop loving. It is to teach them to love, to remember, and to cherish in new ways. Laura Davis reminds grievers, "Memory is not a photographic rendering of our history; it is a collage of images, feelings, perspectives, and fragments that we piece together to form a coherent perception of our past. We create stories about our lives, and as we tell those stories to ourselves—and to others—they become embedded in our sense of personal history."[18]

The goal of a mutual-help group is *not* to help people forget. It is to help them remember realistically. To help them revisit their memories in loving ways.

The goal of a mutual-help group is to give people permission to grieve.

Thanatologist at the University of Memphis, Robert Neimeyer (1998), echoes the growing distrust of reliance on stage thinking:

> As human beings struggling with seemingly inhuman demands, we all too often find ourselves caricatured in the overly simple portrayal of grief offered by traditional "stage" theories of adaptation to loss. Not only do these theories seem strangely anonymous in their description of supposedly universal symptoms of grief and phases of emotional reaction, but they also seem to miss the particulars of our struggle, and its embeddedness in a life that is uniquely our own.[19]

Many will come to the group having been told they *have to do* their grief work in a prescribed way, with the end goal being "recovery," or risk being labeled abnormal or pathological. Some will come believing they need "Remedial Grief 101."

As a mutual-help group facilitator, you do not have to set grievers straight about the theoretical limitations of stage thinking. Remind group members that everyone grieves *uniquely.* To illustrate this, ask group members to look at their thumbs. Then say, "There are 6 billion people on planet Earth. Not one of them has a thumbprint like yours. If God went to all that trouble to make your thumbprint unique, why would your grief be like someone else's?"

Permission-ing

One of the important gifts of facilitators in mutual-help groups is helping participants receive "permission" to do thorough grief work and permission to avoid easy answers. (See permission handout in chapter 3, page 52.)

In order to do thorough grief work, grievers need companions as they attempt to "fit the pieces" together and as God works to "knit" their pieces into wholeness. Sometimes grievers need companions as they attempt to reconcile their grief stories with the grief stories of others in their families.

Thorough grief work is one of life's most demanding tasks. Thorough grief work is the toughest psychological and spiritual work an individual will ever do.

One of the most important things you can do is to give permission to participants to share their grief. As Victoria Alexander grieved in isolation for her father, she concluded that every griever has three essential needs:

- To find the words for the loss
- To say the words aloud
- To know that the words have been heard[20]

First, finding words to accurately portray grief can be like finding a needle in a haystack. "Words cannot begin to describe what I am experiencing," one widow complained. In reality, words do fail us at times of grief. But a griever tests and tries on words like a person stringing beads—one word at a time, until slowly the first sentence is composed. That sentence, however sloppy, jagged, or illogical, becomes a bridge between the griever and the one who wants to help.

Mutual-help groups give grievers time to compose and try out sentences. In our society, we are in such a hurry that we don't give grievers time to frame sentences. Too many would-be "helpers" race in and, in essence, "put words in the grievers' mouths." Grievers generally have lots of sentences with huge gaps in them. Facilitators need to be patient and attentive with the spaces between the words.

Second, grievers do need to say the words aloud—even when those words make others uncomfortable. I often urge participants who are struggling with words, "Just tell us the way you are thinking it, and we will sort it out." Sometimes, almost Scrabble-style, the words tumble out. In some families and in many social circles, workplaces, even churches, death is a taboo experience best kept to oneself. "We don't talk about it." Soon, grievers may conclude that no one really wants to hear about their experiences. Some may initially have a hard time believing that you and others in the group really want to hear their words, to ponder their experiences.

Grief needs to be verbalized. I may presume that I know what you are feeling, but I do not. And I never will unless you tell me. Sometimes words evoke laughter—only because they are so fresh, honest, or unadorned. More than once I have acknowledged, "Well, I have never heard it put quite that way before."

Two things happen when people string words. First, the struggle to verbalize—and the courage to be honest—may jump-start another group member's word search. Grievers recognize in another griever's words their own experiences. "You too?" or "So I am not the only one!"

Sometimes a person's words are so elegant that they become a quotation passed on to others. Take a moment and ponder the words of C. S. Lewis, penned after the death of his close friend Charles Williams: "No event has so corroborated my faith in the next world as Williams did simply by dying. When the idea of death and the idea of Williams thus met in my mind, it was the idea of death that was changed."[21]

The next great helpful quotation to a generation of grievers could come from someone in the mutual-help group you are facilitating.

Third, grievers need to know that their words have been heard. Too many have to say, "Would you just hear me out?" Listening does not mean that a leader accepts everything—but leaders do listen. Remember the question, If a tree falls in the forest and no one hears it, was there a sound? Well, if a griever grieves but no one hears, has there been grief?

Something wonderful happens when someone authentically listens to our words; when someone listens all the way to the end of our sentences; when someone does not immediately thrust a tissue into our face; when someone is comfortable with our silences.

The goal

The goal in the mutual-help group is not to have a "nice" support group but to provide a caring environment in which grief can be verbalized and expressed, received and honored, and thus permissioned. One way to do that is to close every session with these words: "My grief counts." You may need to repeat that phrase several times. "My grief counts." Then ask members to turn to another participant and to say with great zeal: "Your grief counts!" As strange as this may seem, this group may be the first place an individual hears that validation and comes to believe it. Then acknowledge the corporate reality of grief: *"Our* grief counts!"

The goal is to do thorough "drain the last drop" grief work in a society that prefers "lite" grief. When I was growing up, at Sunday dinner, I could always tell the difference between the "made-from-scratch" cakes and the mix cakes. Some Saturdays my mother was just too busy. Family members, employers, coworkers, and friends may become impatient for a griever to "get on with it" so that they can "get over it."

The goal is not to get over this death. The goal is to reconcile with this unchangeable loss and to integrate it into our lives.

Talking about grief is a lot like playing Scrabble, at least in the first moment when all the letters get dumped out. The task is to make a word out of all those letters. The griever's task is to make sense of all the emotions and the interactions with others' grief or grieflessness.

Mutual-help grief groups are important because some of us do not feel comfortable sharing our grief—even with those we love the most. Some grievers, who are very public with grief, assume that those who are not sharing are *not* grieving. In too many cases, the grief goes undercover or is camouflaged.

Most families have assigned roles in the drama of grief.

- **The strong griever.** It's not uncommon to overhear grievers being told, "Now you've got to be strong." Sometimes, it's personalized: "You've got to be strong for [Name/Relational Title]." This is particularly true for males. Society is reluctant to give males permission to grieve. As a result, many become the *quiet* griever in the family. "He doesn't talk about it." If the strong griever is not talking, he or she probably is not listening either.

- **The auditor griever.** This participant takes it upon himself or herself to "audit" the grief (or ungrief) of others. This can be a great way to avoid doing his or her own grief work.
- **The commentator griever.** This individual does color commentary on (as in professional sports) or analyzes every family member's grief expression and progress. The group may be a time for participants to acknowledge these persons in their lives.

A reminder from Francis of Assisi

Anytime you feel incompetent or ill equipped or overwhelmed, spend some time with these words of Francis of Assisi. In fact, I would suggest that you prepare for each session by prayerfully reviewing these words:

Lord, make me an instrument of your peace!
Where there is hatred, let me sow love;
Where there is injury, pardon;
Where there is doubt, faith;
Where there is despair, hope;
Where there is sadness, joy.
O divine master,
Grant that I may not so much seek
To be consoled as to console,
To be understood as to understand,
To be loved as to love.
For it is in giving that we receive,
It is in pardoning that we are pardoned,
And it is in dying
That we are born to eternal life.[22]

The first casualty at the scene of the World Trade Center was fire chaplain Mychal Judge. Ironically, he would have been the one to whom so many families would have turned in their distress after September 11. Previously, Judge had walked fire families through so many losses. Mychal Judge is known for his four-sentence prayer:

Lord, take me where You want me to go.
Let me meet whom You want me to meet.
Help me say what You want me to say.
And keep me from getting in Your way![23]

What a superb prayer for facilitators of mutual-help grief groups.

NOTES

1. Victoria Alexander, *Words I Never Thought to Speak: Stories of Life in the Wake of Suicide* (New York: Lexington Books, 1991), 120.
2. Fanny J. Crosby, "Rescue the Perishing," in *Sing to the Lord* No. 713.
3. Dennis Smith, *Report from Ground Zero: The Story of the Rescue Efforts at the World Trade Center* (New York: Viking, 2002), 338.
4. Helen Wilson Harris, "Congregational Care for the Chronically Ill, Dying, and the Bereaved," *Family Ministry* 14, no. 1 (Spring 2000): 31.
5. Eric Schlosser, "A Grief Like No Other," *The Atlantic Monthly,* September 1997, 50.
6. Dietrich Bonhoeffer, *Life Together,* trans. John W. Doberstein (New York: Harper and Row, 1954), 97.
7. Peter J. Liuzzi, *With Listening Ears* (New York: Paulist Press, 2001), 70.
8. Ethel May Baldwin and David Benson, *Henrietta Mears and How She Did It* (Ventura, Calif.: Regal Books, 1966), 99.
9. Geoffrey Perret, *Eisenhower* (New York: Random House, 1999), 603.
10. Liuzzi, *With Listening Ears,* 70.
11. Zach Thomas, *Healing Touch: The Church's Forgotten Language* (Louisville, Ky.: Westminster/John Knox Press, 1994), 87.
12. Pamela Rosewell, *The Five Silent Years of Corrie ten Boom* (Grand Rapids: Zondervan, 1986), 25.
13. Rudolph Grantham, *Lay Shepherding* (Valley Forge, Penn.: Judson, 1980), 25.
14. Ibid., 64.
15. Curtis Holland, quoted in Helen Wilson Harris, "Congregational Care for the Chronically Ill, Dying, and the Bereaved," *Family Ministry* 14, no. 1 (Spring 2000): 33.
16. Wilkie Au, *The Enduring Heart: Spirituality for the Long Haul* (New York: Paulist Press, 2000), 53.

17. Hope Edelman, *Motherless Daughters: The Legacy of Loss* (New York: Addison-Wesley, 1994), 5.

18. Laura Davis, *I Thought We'd Never Talk Again* (New York: HarperCollins, 2002), 7.

19. Robert A. Neimeyer, *Lessons of Loss: A Guide to Coping* (New York: McGraw-Hill/Primis Custom Publishing, 1998), 83.

20. Alexander, *Words I Never Thought to Speak,* ix.

21. C. S. Lewis, preface to *Essays Presented to Charles Williams*, by Dorothy Sayers, et al. (Grand Rapids: William B. Eerdmans, 1966), xiv.

22. Quoted in Michael Ford, *Father Mychal Judge: An Authentic American Hero* (New York: Crossroad, 2002), 162.

23. Mychal Judge, quoted in Harold Ivan Smith, *When You Don't Know What to Say* (Kansas City: Beacon Hill Press of Kansas City, 2002), 7.

What Makes the Mutual-Help Group Approach Unique?

Many of the principles and activities in a mutual-help group are found in other grief groups. However, the essential difference is the belief that we can help each other. Maybe you've heard the story from the Special Olympics in Seattle. In a particular race all of the participants were Down syndrome children. At some point, one runner fell. When he cried out, the other runners stopped, turned around, and then went back and helped him up. Then they all walked arm in arm toward the finish line.

The goal is not to help a griever "survive." The purposes of a mutual-help grief group are outlined in an analysis of grief developed by Wilke Au.[1]

1. Recognizing and acknowledging the painful loss.
2. Staying with all the different feelings stirred up by that loss until they are quieted.
3. Ritualizing through some symbolic action our letting go of what has been lost.
4. Moving ahead with our plans, hopeful that new life and joy can be ours in the future.

I would add a fifth:

5. Inviting God to "Emmanuel," to "be with us" in our seasons of grief. Emmanuel means "God with us."

As Wilkie Au observed, "The mystery of the incarnation celebrates the fact that God was not content to love humankind from afar, but drew near to love us close-up."[2] Thus we are not content to support grievers "from afar" but from close-up too.

Mayne, whose father suicided, points out that although grievers want answers to the questions, God does not deliver answers. In fact, "there are no answers. Instead, he gives himself,"[3] and He often discloses himself in the wise words of other grievers and the care of a grace-hearted facilitator.

This reality is demonstrated in the great deal of space in scripture given to the death of Lazarus and Jesus' grief for His friend and His compassion for Lazarus's sisters, Mary and Martha. Scripture provides a realistic portrayal. Mary and Martha are hardly polite with Jesus' feelings when they say, "Lord, . . . if you had been here, [our] brother would not have died" (John 11:21, 32). In fact, this chapter gives permission for authentic grief in the disclosure that Jesus "was deeply moved . . . and troubled" (v. 33).

If Jesus had permission to be "moved and troubled," so do the participants in this mutual-help group. This passage is not coincidentally included in the New Testament. It is deliberately included as guidance. It is included, I believe, as a permission to grieve. Repeatedly, Jesus went off into desert places to be alone, but He did His grief "front and center" with Mary and Martha and in front of the large crowd of Jews.

Some may explain their presence in the group by saying, "I am here because my spouse needs help. I am here to support him or her." Some cannot believe that they will ever be reoriented, let alone "surprisingly" reoriented. The grief is too overwhelming at the moment. For some, life is no longer livable.

I find the story of Elijah predicting rain a valuable resource. When he asked his servant to go check the skies, the servant reported the absence of any rain clouds, "nothing there" (1 Kings 18:43). Elijah sends him back seven times to scour the horizon for any hint of rain. Finally, the servant reports, "A cloud as small as a man's hand is rising from the sea" (v. 44). And it rained! Our task as leaders is to scour the horizon for the first hint of hope. As in this story it will not be a great thundercloud—only "a cloud as small as a man's hand."

The leader repeatedly points to a hope cloud on the horizon—the hope of being surprised by God's care. In the words of C. S. Lewis, there will come moments that a griever will be "surprised by joy." I suspect for some the term "ambushed by joy" may be more accurate.

What makes a mutual-help grief group distinctive?

1. The insistence that grief is not prescribed into some notion of stages. We do not jump through "hoops" in grief or wander through predictable stages.
2. The griever must actively pay attention to do grief work.

3. Grievers need permission to grieve thoroughly and creatively in a grief-challenged culture that privatizes and discourages grief and disenfranchises the griever.

The design of the sessions

Each session has material designed around a particular focus:

Session 1	Getting acquainted with other participants and their grief narratives
Session 2	Capturing our relationship and loss in pictures
Session 3	Finding permission to grieve in a "grief-lite" society
Session 4	Developing an attitude of stillness
Session 5	Recognizing an array of choices grievers face
Session 6	Developing the gifts of gratitude

The exercises and experiences in each session are designed to introduce the theme and to give grievers ways to incorporate it into their grief work (and grief is work).

Each unit has most if not all of these elements:

Scripture. A brief passage of scripture is presented to the griever as an opportunity for reflection based on his or her personal loss experience. As leader, you may want to read the scripture aloud and then ask participants to read their paraphrases.

Questions. The questions are designed to link the theme and the resources provided for the group's use. In preparing for the session, you may think of other questions. The group may not have time to consider all the questions. If the group is lively engaging a particular question, you may want to "hang out" there for a while longer.

Work for a smooth transition from the discussion on one question to the next question rather than, "Enough about that—let's move on to the next question."

Checking in. A participant may recognize God's action in their own grief through stories and insights shared by others in this group. For some, the "Aha!" moment may not come within the group but later in the week or even after the group has concluded. Take some time early in each session to review the previous week's focus. Ask: **In reference to last week's session, what have you been thinking about?*** One by-product is that participants receive compliments when someone says, "I have been thinking about something Karen said last week. Her insight really helped me."

A song. Grievers have often given their grief "a voice" in music. Some of the great hymns and gospel song texts have been written by grievers, such as "Day by Day," written by Caroline Sandell-Berg after witnessing her father's death, or Horatio Spafford's "It Is Well with My Soul," written after the drownings of his four daughters.

One creative way to deal with these lyrics is to invite participants to rewrite certain words or phrases—without paying particular attention to cadence. In point, we will be reading the words—not singing them (although some groups may want to sing the song). For example, in the lyrics of "Day by Day," a participant might reword "Strength I find to meet my trials here" as "Strength I find to meet my *grief's demands."* (You will need to give permission to sidestep rhyme and cadence. However, be surprisable—someone might make an incredible "fit.")

Some groups may sing. Or you may want to bring in a CD player and play a CD of the song while participants follow along.

Words of hope. Some grievers have had the gift of writing words from their experience that bring great comfort to other grievers. We are comforted by wise words from other grievers. (In chapter 5, you will find a selection of quotes to use in the group.)

Closing. Time frameworks must be honored, particularly for those in the group who have young children. Some grievers will be clock driven. As leader, you will need to

- ✓ be attentive to the clock,
- ✓ start on time,
- ✓ end on time. To do this, you may need to say, "I am going to ask you to hold that thought for our next session."

---

*Throughout sessions, the words to be spoken by the facilitator will be displayed in boldface type.

Prayer. In each session, I have selected a scripture fragment that I believe to be "griever-friendly." These "lifesavers" may bring some buoyancy to a grief-challenged devotional life. Rather than long scriptures, I have reworded some. By repeating each scripture fragment several times, the griever will allow it to sink into his or her mind in a way a longer passage will not. The psalmist—who knew a great deal about grief and loss—observed, "I have hidden your word in my heart that I might not sin against you" (Ps. 119:11). Grievers can store these scripture fragments for future recall and comfort. For example, if a griever wakes up in the middle of the night, the week's scripture sentence can be a wonderful resource. The psalmist reported, "On my bed I remember you; I think of you through the watches of the night" (63:6).

Ask participants for prayer requests each week: "How can we help pray for you this week?" Remind participants they do not have to share details; indeed, a participant may not be ready to disclose details. But something happens when we enlist others to pray for anxieties in the grief season.

Suppose someone says, "Pray for my relationship with my son, John"? With some groups, the leader might feel comfortable saying, "Who would like to pray for this request?" But remember, there will be differences in people's comfort zones with praying publically. Some people do not or will not pray in public. Remember also that some grievers now question the value of prayer.

Group activity. In each session, there is a suggested group experience. These are designed to engage the "right brains" or the more creative aspects of our minds. The purpose of each group activity is to jump-start thinking.

NOTES

1. Wilke Au, *The Enduring Heart: Spirituality for the Long Haul* (New York: Paulist Press, 2000), 33.

2. Ibid., 116.

3. Michael Mayne, *Pray, Love, Remember* (London: Darton, Longman, and Todd, 1998), 49.

Registration Form

Please Print

My name is ____

I am grieving for [Name] ______________________________

[Relationship: spouse/son/father/daughter/mother]

Who died on [date] ______________________________

I have come to this mutual-help group because

In case a group needs to be canceled or rescheduled, you can contact me at

Name: ____

Address: ____

City: ____

Telephone: Business ________________ Residence ______

E-mail address: _____________________________________

Getting Off to a Good Start

Length

Ideally the mutual-help grief group should meet for 90 minutes. However, many groups will meet for 60 minutes. In either case, it is important that you start and end on time. Expect some individuals to come 15 to 30 minutes early and others to arrive at starting time.

Place

It is important to have a good environment in which to meet. The more comfortable the seating, the more conducive to a good learning setting. I would suggest sitting in a circle. Make certain everyone can see the faces of the other members of the group. For some exercises, you will need tables set up outside the circle of chairs.

While many groups will meet in a church setting, others will meet in someone's home. The leader will want to be alert to factors in the room that can become distractive, particularly temperature and lighting. A ringing telephone or a loud television/CD player in another part of the house can be disruptive to the work of the group.

Ask participants to turn off cell phones for the duration of the session.

If this group meets in a church, possibly some participants who do not attend your church may be unfamiliar with the location of bathrooms, convenient parking, and so on. You may want to have a greeter at the main entrance. If the group meets during Sunday School, make sure regular greeters know where the group is meeting.

Timing

Some groups will meet during the week; others, in churches, will meet during church programming or in Christian education.

Approach

Most mutual-help groups will meet for six or seven weeks. It is also possible to do this material in a weekend conference or retreat format. As a backup you should have the room reserved for an additional week in case you need to reschedule due to inclement weather.

Sign-ins

Although you may ask that individuals preregister or sign up for the class, some may come at the last minute. Because some are unsure about how they will fit in the group, it is important to either greet them personally or have a greeter welcome them at the door. Direct them to the registration table. As facilitator introduce yourself: **I am . . .** Then add a phrase, such as: **I am so glad you have come today/tonight . . .**

Closed group

After the second meeting of the group, it is considered closed to new participants. To add new participants disrupts the group process. Hopefully, you will already have dates for the next session and preregister those who would like to attend.

Name tags

Name tags are important because they personalize interaction: "You know, something that Mary said really touched me." Moreover, even after the group has been meeting for several weeks, grievers have so much on their minds that they cannot always remember a name and that can be embarrassing. Continue to use name tags.

Refreshments

Grieving people will appreciate light refreshments—coffee or hot water for tea or (given the season) punch or hot-spice tea. Some groups provide cookies or fresh fruit. Ask for volunteers to bring refreshments. Refreshments can be conversation jump starters.

How to open

The opening moments of a group can be critical to establishing an environment for good group work. I recommend starting with several calming-down moments (possibly with soft instrumental background music on a CD player). Many grievers rush in to the group after a busy day and need moments for their souls to catch up with their bodies.

Offer a prayer inviting God to be with you in this place.

How to close

Ask participants to stand and join hands to form a circle. Ask them to bow their heads. Then say: **If anyone has a word or phrase they would like to express, do so now.** Close the group with prayer. Ask participants to take a step toward the center of the circle (this tightens the circle). Ask them to take another step toward the center (again tightening the circle). Ask them to take one more step—at this point everyone will be scrunched together, shoulder to shoulder. Say: **This is the Texas hug. Consider yourself hugged. See you next week.**

Remember some people do not like to be hugged; for others this will be one of the most meaningful aspects of the group.

Standing around

At the first session some participants will leave immediately on dismissal; others will choose to stay and talk. As leader, do not schedule yourself in such a way that you have to dash out the door to your next commitment. Some wonderful slices of conversation are exchanged in such moments, particularly if the coffeepot is still plugged in.

Prayer

No doubt you've heard the phrase "Prayer changes things" or this statement: "More things are wrought by prayer than this world dreams of." What you may not know is that this last sentence was written by Alfred, Lord Tennyson after the death of his close friend.

One thing that may make this group different from other groups—secular groups—is the unapologetic use of prayer. As a leader, you do not have to be a "prayer warrior," but it is important for participants to know that you will be praying for them during the course of this small group.

Arrange for a prayer intercessor to pray for your group, possibly while your group is meeting. You might want to provide a list of participants' first names or initials.

As you close a session, you may ask if individuals have prayer requests. Initially, people may be hesitant to offer publicly a request by name, but some may ask you in private to pray for a need. Sometimes all it takes is for one person to "break the ice," and others will join. You might ask: **How can we pray for you this week?**

Remember, many grievers cannot pray. Many feel great guilt for not praying. Some have issues with God: If God is so all-powerful, how come He didn't prevent a loved one's death? Some may have prayed diligently for a healing only to have their loved one die. Share this wonderful word from Reg Johnson: "God never chides his children for being children." God realizes that you do not understand why.

An optional way to close the session is with group prayer. Stand in a circle and join hands. Ask participants to bow their heads and close their eyes. Ask: **Does anyone want to offer a word about tonight's session?** You may hear "hope," "help," "peace." As you close, remind God that the people in the circle are very brave to come to a group. Ask God to take them from this session in peace. Then add: **And bring them back to this circle next week.**

One idea for personalizing prayer is this: Before the group starts, place the pupil's book in your left hand. Now place your right hand on top of it. Ask the Lord to bless you in leading this group. Ask Him to make the material come alive and to help you not become a "slave" to the script but to be open to those wonderful moments when He will seem close.

As a facilitator, pray for participants between sessions. Use the registration forms. Take a moment and pray for each one, and as you do, recall each individual's face.

Options

There is more material included in each session than can be accomplished—this is done to accommodate groups that will meet for 90 minutes as well as groups that will meet for 60 minutes. As a leader, you may decide that some things are essentials and others are options for each week. In leading groups for almost a decade, I have learned that resources I think will work—or that have worked with previous groups—may bomb with this group or in this session. Feel free to choose from optional resources.

Snowflakes

You may want to purchase some paper snowflakes and pass them out to the group. Give them time to study the snowflakes. Ask them to write their deceased loved ones' names on the snowflakes.

Ask: **What is wrong with this snowflake?** Answer: **They are mass-produced and uniform. In reality, there are no two identical snowflakes—similar, but unique. Although it takes millions of snowflakes to make a snowball, yet none of the snowflakes are identical.** This exercise is another way—like the thumbprint—to remind participants of the uniqueness of grief.

Balloons

Sometimes powerful concepts can be captured or symbolized through simple things, such as a balloon. At some point, you may want to ask participants: **Is there something you would like to let go of?** Could be something someone has said—intentionally or unintentionally—or something someone has done or failed to do. You can give a participant time to "name" the item or allow it to go unsaid. Pass out the balloons, and ask each participant to select one. Ask them to stretch the balloons, commenting that grief has a way of stretching an individual. Say: **Now think about something you need today/tonight to let go of. Ask God to help you release it.** After a pause, add these words: **Take your balloon and inflate it, and as you blow your breath into it, look at how large this small balloon has become. Holding your balloon tightly in one hand,**

place your other hand on top of the balloon and ask God to help you let go of whatever this balloon symbolizes. Pause a moment.

Some of us are controllers who like to release it a little at a time. We think we can manage it. But have you ever had a balloon pop in your face? The other alternative is to say, "God, I offer You this hurt. Help me to let go of it." Now raise your balloon over your head and let go! Released balloons will fly across the room. Expect some laughter. Ask: **What does this experience say to you?** Ask them to retrieve their deflated balloons to take with them as a reminder of the need to let go.

A Letter to Send to Participants After the First Meeting

Will a participant return? Sending a letter (computer generated) to each participant generally improves the rate of return. Below is a sample you could use or modify. You may choose to call participants sometime in the week following the first session.

Today is [date].

I wanted to drop a note to you following the first meeting of our mutual-help grief group.

You now have some idea of how the group will function. It is a unique program to give individuals a safe place to share important grief work. Admittedly, at times it is challenging, but we are a circle of learners. Each participant has something to contribute. We need one another's wisdom and courage.

Sometimes the first session can seem overwhelming. But hopefully some seeds were planted to help you. I am hoping you will join us for the remaining weeks.

I admire your courage in being willing to give attention to your grief work. It would be so easy to pull the covers over your head and pretend that grief will go away. In our culture, it is so tempting to do "grief lite." Some of the bravest people in our city participate in this group. And *you* are one of those brave people.

Hope to see you next ________, at ______ A.M./P.M., when the group again meets.

Signed,

[Your Name]

Session 1: Getting Acquainted

Focus

Getting acquainted with other participants and their grief narratives

Before the Session

- Recheck the church calendar to make certain that no one else is scheduled to use this room.
- Make sure you have prepared sufficient copies of the handouts.*
- Arrive early to prepare the room and to greet early arriving participants.
- Check the temperature for comfort in the room.
- Make sure the room is clean and tidy.
- Arrange chairs in a circle.
- Review your materials for the session.
- Set up the registration table, and lay out name tags and markers.
- If you have a flip chart or bulletin board, write out one of the quotations that you have found helpful in chapter 5.

Welcome

Welcome the group.

Music interlude

Take 60 to 90 seconds to listen to a soft piece of praise music that will help people focus on the group's work.

Prayer

Word of introduction

Briefly tell about yourself—your grief narrative—and how God has prepared you to facilitate the group.

---

*Printable versions of the handouts, classified by the chapters in which they are found, are available on *The Grief Care Kit* CD.

Guidelines

Pass out the "Guidelines for Group Participation" handout sheet, Resource 9. Ask participants to follow along as you read the guidelines. Remember, some grieving participants may have difficulty with reading. After the reading ask: **Does anyone have any questions about the group?**

Scripture

One of the ways a mutual-help grief group differs from other grief support groups is that each session will include spiritual exercises that have particular meaning for grievers. Today/Tonight we begin with a psalm phrase that has been prayed, no doubt, by millions of grievers: "Out of the depths I cry to you, O LORD . . . hear my voice" (Ps. 130:1-2).

Repeat this with me. (Quote the verses.)

Let's take a couple of minutes to let these words speak to us. Would you place both feet on the floor? Put your hands on your lap. Make sure your back is straight. Now close your eyes and inhale slowly, then exhale. Breathe in; breathe out. (Repeat this several times.) **As you breathe in softly say these words in your mind: "Out of the depths I cry to you."**

Hold the breath. (Wait a few seconds.) **Now exhale.** (Repeat.)

As you inhale think of the words, "Out of the depth I cry to you."

(Breathe in and out several times.)

Now as you breathe out, think of these words, "O LORD . . . hear my voice." Exhale thinking, "O LORD . . . hear my voice." (Repeat.) **Breathe in; breathe out, thinking, "O LORD . . . hear my voice."**

Let's put these two phrases together. Breathe in on "Out of the depths I cry to you." Hold that breath just a moment. Now exhale, "O LORD . . . hear my voice." (Repeat three times.)

Open your eyes.

Ask: **What did you feel as you thought on this psalm fragment?** (Possibly someone will report: "I felt calm or peaceful." Some may not feel anything initially.)

Introductions

We are going to take some time to introduce ourselves. I would like you to share with us this information (Use the wording that follows to prepare beforehand a card for each participant): (Read from the card.)

My name is ______________________________.

My loved one [Name] ______________ died [date] ___________.

If I had to describe my grief experience in a word or phrase, it would be _____________________________________.

The reason I have come to this mutual-help group is ____________ ____.

I will pass the cards around. Whoever volunteers to go first, we will go around the circle from that volunteer's right. Who would like to go first?

It may be difficult for some participants to answer these questions. Do not be in a hurry. If you become emotional and cannot talk, we will come back to you.

After each participant answers, the facilitator adds: **We welcome you to this group.**

When all participants have shared, say: **You are very courageous to confront your grief. Take a moment and look around the circle. You are seated with brave people. I believe that something extraordinary will happen within this circle in the next six weeks.**

One of our goals is to "receive" one another's grief narrative. We can do that by talking about our experiences as grievers. Today/Tonight I want us to think about some common things experienced by grievers. I will ask a question; then after a moment to reflect on it, I want someone to respond. Then others will have opportunity to respond to the question too.

Questions

You do not have to use all of the questions. Sometimes, a particular question is a "dud." Give the group a little time to think about it.

If no one responds, go on to the next question. (Repeat each question twice.)

Question 1 **What has been the most difficult aspect of your grief?**

Question 2 **What is the most insane or outrageous thing anyone has said to you?**

Question 3 **Who has disappointed you? Who has not "come through" for you?**

Question 4 **Who has surprised you?**

Question 5 **What is the best advice you have been given?**

Question 6 **What is the worst advice you have been given?**

Question 7 **What are you learning about grief and loss?**

Question 8 **How are you experiencing God in your season of grief?**

Question 9 **What would you most hope to get out of participating in this group?**

Song

Each week we will listen to/sing a song. Many of our great hymns and gospel songs were written by grieving persons. Listen to this hymn. (Play CD; pass out Hymn Text 1.)*

Day by Day

Day by day, and with each passing moment,
Strength I find to meet my trials here.
Trusting in my Father's wise bestowment,
I've no cause for worry or for fear.
He whose heart is kind beyond all measure
Gives unto each day what He deems best,
Lovingly its part of pain and pleasure,
Mingling toil with peace and rest.

—Caroline V. Sandell-Berg (*Sing to the Lord,* 105)

*See page 5 for instructions about accessing audio and text files on CD.

Sandell-Berg wrote these words after watching her father fall from a ship and drown. What word or phrase in the hymn text "speaks" to you?

A reflection

It is my hope that in these next weeks you will find this group a safe space to bring your grief. My hope is that this will be *mekom hanekhama*—the Hebrew for "a safe place to do the necessary work of grief." You possibly have had the experience of trying to talk about your grief but having someone look at you as if you were speaking a foreign language. In this group we all speak a language called grief. The question we will repeatedly consider is, "How can I give my grief its voice?"

Words of hope

I would like to share some healing words of hope from author Frank Peretti. (Pass out Quote 1.)

> "God does not waste an ounce of our pain or a drop of our tears; suffering doesn't come our way for no reason, and He seems especially efficient at using what we endure to mold our character. If we are malleable, He takes our bumps and bruises and shapes them into something beautiful."
>
> —Frank Peretti, *The Wounded Spirit,* 183

What do Peretti's words say to you?

After group members have shared, say: **Each week, we will pass out one of these "refrigerator" quotations. You might want to tape it on your refrigerator so that from time to time during this next week, it will be a reminder of God's love for you. Also, this quote may be helpful for family members or friends. You may want to photocopy it to share with someone.**

Closing prayer

How can we help pray for you this week? Does anyone have a special prayer request? Wait a moment for them to respond before asking participants to stand and join hands. **God, You have**

brought us together in this mutual-help grief group. Thank You for each individual standing in this circle. Find ways to remind them of Your love. Give us strength sufficient for the demands of each day of this week. And bring us back to this circle next week. Amen.

Option

You may ask the group to close by saying the Lord's Prayer.

Closing affirmation

Before we go, I want you to repeat with me: "My grief counts." Let's try it again. "My grief counts." Now put an exclamation mark on the end. "My grief counts!" Turn to another participant and say: "*Your* grief counts!"

See you next week.

Session 2: Making Special

Focus

Capturing our relationship with loss in pictures

Before the session

- Recheck the church calendar to make certain that no one else is scheduled to use this room.
- Arrive early to prepare the room and to greet early arriving participants.
- Check the temperature for comfort in the room.
- Make sure the room is clean and tidy.
- Arrange the seating in a circle.
- Review that you have sufficient materials for the session.
- Set up the registration table, and lay out name tags and markers.
- If you have a flip chart or bulletin board, you might want to write a quotation that you have found helpful in chapter 5.

Welcome

Welcome the group.

Music interlude

Take 60 to 90 seconds to listen to a soft piece of praise music that will help people focus on the group's work.

Prayer

Checking in

It is good to see you again. Let's go around the group and reintroduce ourselves. Briefly tell your name and the name of your deceased one. Then tell us what kind of a week you had. Who would like to go first?

Scripture

Each week we will have an opportunity to reflect on a verse

of scripture that many grievers find helpful in their losses. As facilitator, read the scripture aloud: **"Do not be anxious about anything, but in everything, by prayer and petition, with thanksgiving, present your requests to God. And the peace of God, which transcends all understanding, will guard your hearts and your minds in Christ Jesus" (Phil. 4:6-7).**

Repeat this with me. (Quote the verses.)

We will take a couple of minutes to let these verses speak to us. Would you place both feet on the floor. Put your hands on your lap. Make sure your back is straight. Close your eyes and inhale slowly, then exhale. Breathe in; breathe out. (Repeat this several times.)

As you breathe in softly, say these words in your mind: "Do not be anxious about anything." Hold the breath. (Wait a few seconds.) **Now exhale.** (Repeat.) **As you inhale, think of the words, "Do not be anxious about anything."**

(Breathe in and out several times.)

Now as you breathe out, think of these words: "but . . . present your requests to God." Exhale thinking, "but . . . present your requests to God." (Repeat.)

Breathe in; breathe out, thinking, "but . . . present your requests to God." Let's put these two phrases together. Breathe in on, "Do not be anxious about anything." Hold that breath just a moment. Now exhale, "but . . . present your requests to God." (Repeat three times.) **Please open your eyes.**

Ask: **What did you feel as you thought of this scripture fragment?** (Be prepared for a wide variety of answers: peace, calm, etc.) Or say: **What came to your mind? What anxieties are you feeling today?** (Answers may include insurance, worrying about paying the bills, etc.)

Activity

You've heard "A picture is worth a thousand words," haven't you? In the last few years there has been an interest in making scrapbooks. Pictures help us remember. Unfortunately, some think the goal of grief is to forget their loved ones. No. It is to remember.

One effective way to help grievers get in touch with their memories is by making collages. A collage is a story—the story of the one you have loved and lost. Today/Tonight we will select pictures, words, and images from magazines to "make a story."

I want you to take a sheet of poster paper (30" x 24") and fold the sheet in half (shortwise). Assume this is a book jacket. On the cover, capture your loved one in pictures from these magazines.

Look through these magazines, and find pictures that tell the stories of your loved one and/or the relationship. This will be something of a photographic quilt. After you have pictures—or words—arrange and paste them onto the poster paper with a glue stick.

Remember, this is a creative experience. There is no right or wrong way to create a collage. Just let your heart and mind be creative. If you don't see some words or phrases, there are markers available for you to use. We will have about [30] minutes to work on these collages, so you do not have to hurry.

(As participants work, some will talk among themselves; others will work alone intently. You may want to play a CD softly in the background.) Twenty minutes into the experience say: **Do not feel that you have to complete your collage tonight. You have about 10 minutes before we come back to the circle.** At 25 minutes into the experience say: **You have 5 minutes before we come back to the circle.**

As facilitator, you may want to work on a collage too.

When participants return to the circle, say: **Please stand the collage on the floor against your kneecaps so everyone in the circle can see it.**

When everyone has returned to the circle, say: **Take a moment and look around the circle at these collages. These are stories. Loving stories. Caring stories.** Allow a couple of minutes for this. Then ask: **Who would like to go first to tell us about your collage?** As the individual finishes, say: **Thank you for sharing your collage and for going first. Who would like to go next?**

Option: An alternative way is to ask participants what they "see" in the collage before the individual explains the collage.

Collage making can be highly emotional. Sometimes a particular picture in a magazine jump-starts a memory. One or two participants may make only a halfhearted attempt to do the collage. But to most participants this may be the way to do *humuhumu,* the Hawaiian word meaning "to knit pieces of their experience together."

When all have shared (or at the end of the session), say: **Open up the poster board to full size.** Point to the half they have worked on and say: **This half represents your past and present. The blank side represents your future. What do you want to take from the past into your future?**

(Based on the number of participants, if all do not get to share their collage, ask them to bring them back next week. As facilitator, stay sensitive to the time.)

I want to suggest two items of "homework." First, show the collage to two people—could be complete strangers. Or leave the collage someplace where other family members or friends can see it. Some grievers find this initiates some interesting dialogue. Second, keep working on the collage, perhaps adding actual photographs to personalize it. Over the next weeks keep your eyes open for something that "belongs" in your collage.

You may wish to ask participants to bring back their collages for the final session to show what they have added.

For the collage exercise you will need the following:

- ✓ Several old magazines per each participant; the more variety, the better to reflect personal interests of the loved one—gardening, sports, decorating, newsmagazines. Also have magazines with religious symbols in them.
- ✓ Glue sticks.
- ✓ Adult-size scissors.
- ✓ A sheet of white poster paper for each participant.
- ✓ A large trash can or trash bag.

Song

Listen to this folk song. (Play CD; pass out Hymn Text 2.)

Precious Memories

(1)

As I travel down life's pathway,
Know not what the years may hold.
As I ponder, hopes grow fonder,
Precious memories flood my soul.

(Refrain)

Precious memories, how they linger,
How they ever flood my soul.
In the stillness of the midnight,
Precious sacred scenes unfold.

(2)

Precious father, loving mother,
Glide across the lonely years.
And old home scenes from my childhood
In fond memory appears.

—Traditional folk song, words by J. B. F. Wright

Memories can be great gifts that we open during our grieving season. What word or phrase in the song text "speaks" to you?

It is my hope that as you work on the collage over these next weeks, you will find this group a safe space to let your memories comfort you. Collages are one of the ways we give grief its voice.

Words of hope

I would like to share with you some wonderful words of hope from Susan Ford Wiltshire, whose brother, John, died in 1993. (Pass out Quote 2.)

> "We were changed by those we love who have left us because we were formed by them while they were here.
>
> "When someone dies or leaves, we have to revisit in new ways the places they inhabited in our hearts. It is not so much that we take part of them into us as that, in their absence, we discover or cultivate a part of us we did not know was there. This

does not compensate for their loss. The loss is still loss, but our creative healing becomes part of their legacy to us."

—Susan Ford Wiltshire, *Athena's Disguises,* 135

What do Susan Ford Wiltshire's words say to you?

After group members have shared, say: **Each week, we will pass out a "refrigerator" quotation. You might want to tape it on your refrigerator so that from time to time during this next week, it will be a reminder of God's love for you. Also, this quote may be helpful for family members or friends. You may want to photocopy it to share with someone.**

Closing prayer

How can we help pray for you this week? Does anyone have a special prayer request? Wait a moment before asking: **Would you stand and join hands? Let's pray: God, You have brought us together in this mutual-help grief group. Thank You for each individual standing in this circle. Find ways to remind them of Your love. Give us strength sufficient for the demands of each day of this week. And bring us back to this circle next week. Amen.**

Option

You may ask the group to close by saying the Lord's Prayer.

Closing affirmation

Before we go, I want you to repeat with me: "My grief counts." "My grief counts." Now put an exclamation mark on the end. "My grief counts!" Turn to another participant and say: *"Your* grief counts!"

See you next week.

Session 3: Finding Permission to Grieve

Focus

Finding permission to grieve in a "grief-lite" society

Before the session

- Arrive early to prepare the room and to greet early arriving participants.
- Check the temperature for comfort in the room.
- Make sure the room is clean and tidy.
- Arrange the seating in a circle.
- Review materials for the session.
- Lay out name tags and markers.
- If you have a flip chart or bulletin board, you might want to write out a quotation that you have found helpful from chapter 5.

Welcome

Welcome the group.

Music interlude

Take 60 to 90 seconds to listen to a soft piece of praise music that will help people focus on the group's work.

Prayer

Checking in

Thank you for coming back for Session 3. Let's take some time to see how our weeks have gone. Who would like to go first?

Scripture

Each week we will have an opportunity to reflect on a verse of scripture that many grievers find helpful in their losses. As facilitator, read the verse aloud: **"[Lord,] according to your love remember me" (Ps. 25:7).**

Repeat this verse with me. (Quote the verse.)

Let's spend a couple of minutes to let this verse speak to us. Would you place both feet on the floor. Put your hands on your lap. Make sure your back is straight. Now close your eyes and inhale slowly, then exhale. Breathe in; breathe out. (Repeat this several times.)

As you breathe in softly, say these words in your mind: "[Lord,] according to your love." Hold the breath. (Wait a few seconds.) **Now exhale.** (Repeat.) **As you inhale, think of the words, "[Lord,] according to your love."**

(Breathe in and out several times.)

Now as you breathe out, think of these words: "remember me." Exhale, thinking, "remember me." (Repeat.)

Let's put these two phrases together. Breathe in on, "[Lord,] according to your love." Exhale, "remember me." (Repeat three times.) **Please open your eyes.**

Ask: **What did you feel as you thought on this psalm fragment?** (Expect a wide variety of answers.)

Activity

This society is one that encourages individuals, "Got something to say . . . then say it!" How many of you have ever said, "I'd like to get something off my chest," or "Thank you for putting in your two cents worth"? In our society, one way people "get things off their chests" is by putting the idea on a bumper sticker. Some stickers you instantly understand; others take a few blocks or a few miles.

Does anyone remember those contests where they ask you to state something in 25 words or less? Bumper stickers do not use a lot of words to get their point across.

We're so busy sometimes people say, "Just give me the short version." Suppose you could say something about grief on a bumper sticker. From your personal experience, what would you want to tell the world about grief?

Take a sheet of blank paper, and fold it in half lengthwise. (Illustrate this.) **Then write that salient point on one side and a sec-**

ond thought on the other. If you mess up, just reverse the paper and start over. In a previous mutual-help grief group, participants wrote, "Our loss is Heaven's gain," and "*Grief* is not for sissies!"

So, what would you like to put on your bumper that would educate others about grief? You will have about 10 minutes for this exercise. Make two bumper stickers, then return to the circle.

When all participants have completed their bumper stickers, ask them to return to the circle.

Ask: **Who would like to share his or her bumper sticker?** Continue until everyone has had a chance to share.

Attributed to the late Sidney Jourard are the words, "To be able to put into words and phrases what others only think is what makes poets and sages." Well, maybe we can say, "To be able to put onto bumper stickers what others only think is what makes poets and sages."

Learning experiences

One of the most important documents for Americans is our Bill of Rights, part of the Constitution. Dr. Alan Wolfelt of the Center for Grief and Loss Transition has developed a list of rights that all grievers have. (Pass out Resource 2, Wolfelt's "Rights for Grievers.") Read the 10 rights aloud. Or go around the circle, and let each participant read one right. When all the rights have been read, take a few moments of silence to reflect on the list.

Then say: **Which right leaped out at you?** or **Which right seems the most important on this list?**

Rights for Grievers

1. I have the right to experience my own unique grief.
2. I have the right to talk about my grief.
3. I have the right to feel a multitude of emotions.
4. I have the right to be tolerant of my physical and emotional and financial limits.
5. I have the right to experience "griefbursts."
6. I have the right to make use of additional ritual.

7. I have the right to embrace my spirituality.
8. I have the right to search for meaning.
9. I have the right to honor my memories.
10. I have the right to move toward my grief and to heal.

Source: Adapted from Alan D. Wolfelt, *The Journey Through Grief, Reflections on Healing* (Fort Collins, Colo.: Companion Press, 1997), 141-43.

If there is time, ask: **Can you think of a right of a griever that is not on the list?**

Questions

Question 1 **In a culture that encourages "Get over it!" or "Get on with your life!" who has given you permission to grieve? Who has encouraged you to pay attention to your grief?**

Question 2 **Who has discouraged your active grief?**

Question 3 **What makes so many people uncomfortable around grievers?**

Question 4 **What is one way you have given yourself permission to grieve?**

Question 5 **If the Lord were in this room, what would He say to you about your grief?**

Question 6 **What are some ways you are giving your grief "a voice"?**

Words of hope

I would like to share with you some wonderful words of hope from Lady Bird Johnson, first lady, 1963-69. Her mother, Minnie, died at Christmastime, 1918, when Lady Bird was six years old. (Pass out Quote 3.)

"People must be given the opportunity to hurt out loud."

—Lady Bird Johnson, in Jan Jarboe Russell, *Lady Bird: A Biography of Mrs. Johnson,* 53

What do Lady Bird Johnson's words say to you?

Song

Each week we will listen to/sing a song. Many of our great hymns and gospel songs were written by grieving persons. Listen to this hymn. (Play CD; pass out Hymn Text 3.)

Does Jesus Care?

(1)

Does Jesus care when my heart is pained
Too deeply for mirth and song,
As the burdens press, And the cares distress,
And the way goes weary and long?

(Refrain)

O yes, He cares; I know He cares!
His heart is touched with my grief.
When the days are weary, The long nights dreary,
I know my Savior cares.

(2)

Does Jesus care when my way is dark
With a nameless dread and fear?
As the daylight fades Into deep night shades,
Does He care enough to be near?

(3)

Does Jesus care when I've said good-bye
To the dearest on earth to me,
And my sad heart aches Till it nearly breaks?
Is it aught to Him? Does He see?

—Frank E. Graeff (*Sing to the Lord*, 574)

Do any of those words "leap out" at you?

Closing prayer

How can we help pray for you this week? Does anyone have a special prayer request? Pause a moment. Then say: **Stand and join hands. God, You have brought us together in this mutual-**

help grief group. Thank You for each individual standing in this circle. Find ways to remind them of Your love. Give us strength sufficient for the demands of each day of this week. And bring us back to this circle next week. Amen.

Option

You may ask the group to close by saying the Lord's Prayer.

Closing affirmation

Before we go, I want you to repeat with me: "My grief counts." Now put an exclamation mark at the end. "My grief counts!" Turn to another participant and say: "*Your* grief counts!"

See you next week.

Session 4: Making Room for Stillness

Focus

Developing an attitude of stillness

Before the session

- Arrive early to prepare the room.
- Check the temperature for comfort in the room.
- Make sure the room is clean and tidy.
- Arrange the seating in a circle.
- Review materials for the session.
- Lay out name tags and markers.
- If you have a flip chart or bulletin board, you might want to write out a quotation that you have found helpful from chapter 5.

Welcome

Welcome the group.

Music interlude

Take 60 to 90 seconds to listen to a soft piece of praise music that will help people focus on the group's work.

Prayer

Checking in

It is good to see you again. What kind of a week have you had? Who would like to go first?

Scripture

This week we are going to work with a prayer phrase from Ps. 46:10: "Be still, and know that I am God." Close your eyes, and silently breathe in on, "Be still, and know." Now exhale. Breathe in on, "Be still, and know." Breathe out. Now breathe in on, "Be still, and know," and exhale on, "that I am God." Breathe

in on, "Be still, and know"; breathe out on, "that I am God." One more time.

Tonight/Today we will do something a little different. Repeat this psalm fragment slowly, each time emphasizing a different word. (Give participants a couple minutes to do this.)

Now one more time, breathe in on, "Be still and know," and breathe out on, "that I am God." What word leaped out at you? (Give time for answers.) **What does this scripture say to you in this grief season?**

Song

Last week we listened to/sang a song. Many of our great hymns and gospel songs were written by grieving persons. Listen to this gospel song. (Play CD; pass out Hymn Text 4.)

What a Friend We Have in Jesus

(1)

What a Friend we have in Jesus,
All our sins and griefs to bear!
What a privilege to carry
Ev'rything to God in prayer!
O what peace we often forfeit,
O what needless pain we bear,
All because we do not carry
Ev'rything to God in prayer!

(2)

Have we trials and temptations?
Is there trouble anywhere?
We should never be discouraged;
Take it to the Lord in prayer.
Can we find a friend so faithful
Who will all our sorrows share?
Jesus knows our ev'ry weakness;
Take it to the Lord in prayer.

(3)

Are we weak and heavy-laden,
Cumbered with a load of care?
Precious Savior, still our Refuge!
Take it to the Lord in prayer.
Do thy friends despise, forsake thee?
Take it to the Lord in prayer.
In His arms He'll take and shield thee;
Thou wilt find a solace there.

—Joseph M. Scriven (*Sing to the Lord,* 625)

Death has a way of challenging all our plans. Ask Joseph Scriven, whose fiancé drowned the night before their wedding. Soon he decided on a "fresh start" and immigrated to Canada. In time, he fell in love again.

Unbelievably, this fiancé died unexpectedly. Joseph changed after that second significant loss. He mourned not only for the women he had loved but also for what "might have been." In despair, he wrote out of his pain the beloved hymn text, "What a Friend We Have in Jesus." Many people know the phrase "all our sins and griefs to bear." Others sing the song without hearing the phrase "and griefs"—plural—until they are grieving.

Joseph added, "O what peace we often forfeit, / O what needless pain we bear." Why? "All because we do not carry / Ev'rything to God in prayer!" Everything? We carry to God everything in the landscape of our grief. There was no "and they all lived happily ever after" ending for Joseph. In fact, he became something of an outcast in his community. There were questions about the circumstances of his death—accident or suicide? But this griever gave the world—and grievers—great counsel: "Take it to the Lord in prayer."

If you could ask Joseph Scriven one question, what would it be?

(For more information, see Kenneth W. Osbeck, *101 Hymn Stories* [Grand Rapids: Kriegel Publications, 1982], 275-77.)

Questions

One of the areas impacted by grief is our ability to pray. Joyce Rupp has written, "Grief has a way of plundering our prayer life, leaving us feeling immobile and empty" (*Praying Our Goodbyes,* [Notre Dame, Ind.: Ave Maria Press, 1988], 79).

Question 1 **How has your prayer life been impacted by grief?**

Question 2 **If someone were to ask "What good does it do to pray?" how would you now respond?**

Question 3 **John Bunyan wrote, "The best prayers are often more groans than words." Do you agree or disagree?**

Question 4 **Joseph Scriven wrote, "What a privilege to carry, / Ev'rything to God in prayer." Are you able to carry *everything* to God in prayer? Or are there certain things about this loss you cannot talk to God about? What do you need to talk to God in prayer about?**

Question 5 **What are some ways we can pray that are not traditional?**

Words of hope

For almost 500 years, grievers have been using a prayer that "covers the waterfront" of our needs. (Pass out Quote 4.)

God, be in my head . . . and in my understanding.
God, be in my eyes . . . and in my looking.
God, be in my mouth . . . and in my speaking.
God, be in my heart . . . and in my thinking.
God, be in my grieving . . . and in my healing.

—Adapted from *Book of Hours* (1514)

This week, I would like you to spend some time praying this prayer.

Closing prayer

How can we help pray for you this week? Does anyone have a special prayer request? Pause a moment. **Would you stand and**

join hands? God, You have brought us together in this mutual-help grief group. Thank You for each individual standing in this circle. Find ways to remind them of Your love. Give us strength sufficient for the demands of each day of this week. And bring us back to this circle next week. Amen.

Option

You may ask the group to close by saying the Lord's Prayer.

Closing affirmation

Before we go, I want you to repeat with me: "My grief counts." Let's try it again. "My grief counts." Now put an exclamation mark on the end. "My grief counts!" Turn to another participant and say: "*Your* grief counts!"

See you next week.

Session 5: Recognizing Choices

Focus

Recognizing an array of choices grievers face

Before the session

- Arrive early to prepare the room.
- Check the temperature for comfort in the room.
- Make sure the room is clean and tidy.
- Arrange the seating in a circle.
- Review materials for the session.
- Set up the registration table, and lay out name tags and markers.
- If you have a flip chart or bulletin board, you might want to write a quotation that you have found helpful in chapter 5.

Welcome

Welcome the group.

Music interlude

Take 60 to 90 seconds to listen to a soft piece of praise music that will help people focus on the group's work.

Prayer

Checking in

Thank you for coming back for Session 5. Let's take some time to talk about how our weeks have gone. Who would like to go first?

Scripture

Each week we have had an opportunity to reflect on a verse of scripture that many grievers find helpful in their losses. As facilitator, read the verse aloud: **"God is our refuge and strength, an ever-present help in trouble" (Ps. 46:1).**

Now close your eyes, and silently pray these words, each time emphasizing a different word. What word leaped out at you?

Place both feet on the floor. Put your hands on your lap. Make sure your back is straight. Close your eyes and inhale slowly, then exhale. Breathe in; breathe out. (Repeat this several times.)

As you breathe in softly, say these words in your mind: "God is our refuge and strength." Hold the breath. (Wait a few seconds.) **Now exhale.** (Repeat.) **As you inhale, think of the words, "God is our refuge and strength."**

(Breathe in and out several times.)

Now as you breathe out, think of these words, "an ever-present help in trouble." Exhale thinking, "an ever-present help in trouble." (Repeat.)

Let's put these two phrases together. Breathe in on, "God is our refuge and strength." Exhale on, "an ever-present help in trouble." (Repeat three times.) **Please open your eyes.**

Ask: **What did you feel as you thought on this psalm fragment?** (Be prepared for a wide variety of answers.)

Activity (Pass out Resource 3.)

On this handout you will find two sentence fragments. At this time focus on the first fragment: "Grief came knocking at my door one day." Turn that fragment over in your mind several times. Then write a poem with at least four more lines. It does not have to rhyme. Do not worry about spelling and punctuation. Just let your creativity flow. You can write more than four lines if you wish. When you are finished writing your first poem, come back to the circle. (Give participants about 8 to 10 minutes to write.)

When everyone has returned to the circle, say: **Who would like to read his or her poem?** Ask participants: **What did you hear in [Name's] poem?** Give them a moment to reflect.

Then ask for another volunteer. Proceed until each one has had a chance to read. (Some may be reluctant to read, discounting their own creativity. This exercise lets them know their words count.)

Would you look at the second fragment: "I keep hoping that one of these days." Turn that fragment over in your mind several times. Write a poem with at least four more lines. It does not have to rhyme. When you have finished, come back to your seat in the circle.

(Repeat the sharing sequence from the first poem. If there is still time, you may want to use one of these exercises.)

Option 1: **Think about some words that characterize your grief experience, such as "pain," "anguish," "betrayal," and so on. There are many others. Let's name five words. Who has a word to suggest?** After they have suggested words, say: **Let's take the following words. Write a poem using these five words at least once.** (Some participants may find this easier than the previous two tasks.) **Again, four or five lines, at least. When you have finished, return to the group.**

Option 2: Ask participants to write three phrases using a total of 10 words (first and second sentences have 3 words each; third sentence has 4 words) that describe their experiences of grief. Read aloud these examples.

Grief came calling.

My child died.

I am trusting God.

Grief is painful.

I am devastated.

God will be faithful.

If there is time, ask participants: **What surprised you in writing these poems?** After they have answered, say: **Let me suggest that you share your words with some family or friends.**

Song

Each week we will listen to/sing a song. Many of our great hymns and gospel songs were written by grieving persons. Listen to this hymn. (Play CD; pass out Hymn Text 5.)

He Keeps Me Singing

There's within my heart a melody.
Jesus whispers sweet and low:
"Fear not, I am with thee; peace, be still,"
In all of life's ebb and flow.

(Refrain)

Jesus, Jesus, Jesus—
Sweetest name I know,
Fills my ev'ry longing,
Keeps me singing as I go.

Luther Bridgers was a popular evangelist and preacher. His spirited new four-verse gospel song "He Keeps Me Singing" was very popular with congregations after it was published in 1910. Tragically, later that year, his wife and three sons died in a fire at his father-in-law's home in Harrodsburg, Kentucky, while they were visiting. In his grief, Bridgers wrote a new fourth verse (Reynolds, William J., Hymns of Our Faith [Nashville: Broadman, 1964], 258).

Tho' sometimes He leads thro' waters deep,
Trials fall across the way,
Tho' sometimes the path seems rough and steep,
See His footprints all the way.

—Luther B. Bridgers (*Sing to the Lord,* 349)

Words of hope (Pass out Quote 5.)

"Remembering the person
I have loved allows me to slowly heal.
Healing does not mean I will forget.
Actually, it means I will remember.
Gently, I will move forward,
never forgetting my past."

—Alan D. Wolfelt, *Creating Meaningful Ceremonies,* 47

Closing prayer

How can we help pray for you this week? Does anyone have a special prayer request? Wait a moment, then ask: **Would you**

stand and join hands. God, You have brought us together in this mutual-help grief group. Thank You for the creativity the participants have expressed tonight. Remind each participant that his or her words count in this season of grief. Find ways to remind each one of Your love. Give us strength sufficient for the demands of each day of this week. And bring us back to this circle next week. Amen.

Option

You may ask the group to close by saying the Lord's Prayer.

Closing affirmation

Before we go, I want you to repeat with me: "My grief counts." Let's try it again. "My grief counts." Now put an exclamation mark on the end. "My grief counts!" Turn to another participant and say: "If my grief counts, so does yours!"

See you next week.

Session 6: Expressing Gratitudes

Focus

Developing the gifts of gratitude

Before the session

- Arrive early to prepare the room.
- Check the temperature for comfort in the room.
- Make sure the room is clean and tidy.
- Arrange the seating in a circle.
- Review materials for the session.
- Lay out name tags and markers.
- If you have a flip chart or bulletin board, you might want to write out a quotation that you have found helpful in chapter 5.

Welcome

Welcome the group.

Music Interlude

Take 60 to 90 seconds to listen to a soft piece of praise music that will help people focus on the group's work.

Prayer

Checking in

Again it is good to see you. Let's go around the group and tell what kind of a week you had. Who would like to go first?

Scripture

Over these weeks we have had an opportunity to reflect on a fragment of scripture that many grievers find helpful in their losses. The fragment for this session is Lam. 3:22-23.

"Because of the LORD's great love we are not consumed, for

his compassions never fail. They are new every morning; great is your faithfulness." Repeat this verse with me. (Quote the verse.)

Let's take a couple of minutes to let this verse speak to us. Would you place both feet on the floor and your hands on your lap. Make sure your back is straight. Now close your eyes and inhale slowly, then exhale. Breathe in; breathe out. (Repeat this several times.)

As you breathe in softly say these words in your mind: "Because of the LORD's great love we are not consumed." Hold the breath. (Wait a few seconds.) **Now exhale.** (Repeat.)

As you inhale think of the words, "Because of the LORD's great love we are not consumed."

(Breathe in and out several times.)

Now as you breathe out, think of these words, "his compassions . . . are new every morning." Exhale, thinking, "his compassions . . . are new every morning." (Repeat.)

Let's put these two phrases together. Breathe in on, "Because of the LORD's great love we are not consumed"; hold that breath. Exhale, "his compassions are . . . new every morning." (Repeat three times.) **Please open your eyes.**

Ask: **What did you feel as you thought on this scripture fragment?** (Be prepared for a wide variety of answers.)

Profile

Some of you can remember that day in Dallas in 1963 as Jackie Kennedy cradled her husband's head in her lap; who can forget that stoic figure in black following her husband's funeral caisson?

On weekends she went to a country home in Virginia, sometimes joined by friends like Tony and Ben Bradlee. Jackie "could not stop reliving those life-changing moments in Dallas." The Bradlees, groping for some kind of response to comfort her, reminded her that she had to think about the future. She was young, might remarry, and perhaps have more children. Although hurt by the remarks, initially Jackie did not respond.

On December 20, she wrote them, "Something you said in

the country stunned me so—that you hoped I would marry again." Jackie declared, "There is one thing you must know. I consider that my life is over and I will spend the rest of it waiting for it really to be over."

To another friend, Jackie lamented, "No one knows what it's like; no one knows what it's like."

(For more information, see Christopher Anderson, *Jackie After Jack* [New York: William Morrow, 1998], 81-87.)

Questions

Question 1 **What do you "hear" in Mrs. Kennedy's words: "I consider that my life is over"? Have you felt that way?**

Question 2 **What are you most dreading about living without your loved one?**

Question 3 **What will you miss most about your loved one? What will you *not* miss?**

Activity

If grievers only focus on what has been lost, they miss the blessing of recognizing what remains. Quite frankly, some gratitudes will be for small items: "For Wilma who has been such a good friend to me." Gratitude audits are essential for thorough grief work. (Pass out Resource 4.) **Today/Tonight I want us to spend some time auditing our gratitudes. This sheet asks you to list a dozen gratitudes. You may not be able to come up with a dozen in the allotted time. Or you may hear another's gratitude and want to include that on your sheet. But take a few moments, and think about what you have to be grateful for. Begin by praying: "God, help me remember what I have to be grateful for."**

Today/Tonight I am grateful for __________________________.

Today/Tonight I am grateful for __________________________.

Today/Tonight I am grateful for __________________________.

Today/Tonight I am grateful for __________________________.

Today/Tonight I am grateful for ______________________.

Today/Tonight I am grateful for ______________________.

Today/Tonight I am grateful for ______________________.

Today/Tonight I am grateful for ______________________.

Today/Tonight I am grateful for ______________________.

Today/Tonight I am grateful for ______________________.

Today/Tonight I am grateful for ______________________.

Today/Tonight I am grateful for ______________________.

Song

Each week we have listened to/sung a song. Many of our great hymns and gospel songs were written by grieving persons. Listen to this hymn. (Play CD; pass out Hymn Text 6.)

It Is Well with My Soul

(1)

When peace like a river attendeth my way,
When sorrows like sea billows roll,
Whatever my lot, Thou hast taught me to say,
"It is well, it is well with my soul."

(Refrain)

It is well with my soul.
It is well, it is well with my soul.

(2)

Tho' Satan should buffet, tho' trials should come,
Let this blest assurance control,
That Christ hath regarded my helpless estate,
And hath shed His own blood for my soul.

(3)

And, Lord, haste the day when the faith shall be sight,
The clouds be rolled back as a scroll,

The trump shall resound and the Lord shall descend.
Even so—it is well with my soul.

—Horatio G. Spafford (*Sing to the Lord,* 554)

Life had become difficult for lawyer Horatio G. Spafford. His real estate holdings were wiped out in the great Chicago fire of 1871; he had lost a son. He decided on a trip to England for his family in the fall of 1873. At the last minute, some professional obligations required his attention, so he sent his wife and their four daughters ahead on the *SS Ville du Havre;* he expected to follow soon thereafter. On November 22, the ship was struck by the British ship *Lochearn* and sank in 12 minutes. His four daughters drowned. After Mrs. Spafford was rescued and after reaching Wales, she cabled him, "Saved alone."

Devastated, Spafford soon sailed for England. It has been thought that when the captain notified him of the ship's reaching the point where his daughters drowned, he wrote the powerful text, "When sorrows like sea billows roll." Rather than focusing on the loss, Spafford wrote of the promise of God's grace. Little wonder that for over a century, "It Is Well" has been a favorite of Christians (Kenneth Osbeck, *101 Hymn Stories* [Grand Rapids: Kriegel Publications, 1982], 127).

Words of hope

I would like to share some wonderful words of hope by Darcie Sims. (Pass out Quote 6.)

> "Right now, you may feel like the scattered pieces of a broken puzzle. Honor that feeling, but also take comfort in knowing that the pieces of a puzzle can be reshuffled, rearranged, and pieced together to form a new picture. As you learn to create a new reality for yourself, temper your expectations with compassion and gentleness.
>
> "Slowly, gently, I have begun to focus on my loved one's life—not the death—and that has made all the difference."
>
> —Darcie Sims, bereaved parent, *Getting Through the Holidays When You've Lost a Loved One,* 7

Note

If in Session 2 you asked participants to bring back their collages, you may have to keep a close watch on the time.

If this is the last session, at this point, give each one a chance to comment on "what I have learned in this mutual-help grief group."

When all participants have had a chance to comment, proceed to the naming ritual (chapter 4).

If you are planning a seventh meeting for a wrap-up, proceed to the closing prayer.

Closing prayer

How can we help pray for you this week? Does anyone have a prayer request? Wait a moment. **God, You have brought us together in this mutual-help grief group. Thank You for each individual standing in this circle. Find ways to remind them of Your love. Bring us back to this circle next week, and give us strength sufficient for the demands of each day. Amen.**

Optional Session: Making Hope

Focus

Nurturing hope seeds in a grief-tinted season

Before the session

- Arrive early to prepare the room.
- Check the temperature for comfort in the room.
- Make sure the room is clean and tidy.
- Arrange the seating in a circle.
- Review materials for the session.
- Set up the registration table and lay out name tags and markers.
- If you have a flip chart or bulletin board, you might want to write out a quotation from chapter 5 that you have found meaningful.

Welcome

Welcome the group.

Music interlude

Take 60 to 90 seconds to listen to a soft piece of praise music that will help people focus on the group's work.

Prayer

Checking in

Thank you for coming back for Session 7. Let's take some time to see how our weeks have gone. Who would like to go first?

Scripture

Each week we will have an opportunity to reflect on a verse

of scripture that many grievers find helpful in their losses. (As facilitator, you may want to read the scripture aloud.)

"'For I know the plans I have for you,' declares the LORD, 'plans to prosper you and not to harm you, plans to give you hope and a future'" (Jer. 29:11). Repeat this verse with me. (Quote the verse.)

Let's spend a couple of minutes letting this verse speak to us. Would you place both feet on the floor. Put your hands on your lap. Make sure your back is straight. Now close your eyes and inhale slowly, then exhale. Breathe in; breathe out. (Repeat this several times.)

As you breathe in softly, say these words in your mind: "'For I know the plans I have for you,' declares the LORD." Hold the breath. (Wait a few seconds.) **Now exhale.** (Repeat.)

(Breathe in and out several times.)

Now as you breathe out, think of these words: "'plans to give you hope and a future.'" Exhale thinking, "'plans to give you hope and a future.'" (Repeat.)

Let's put these two phrases together. Breathe in on, "'For I know the plans I have for you' declares the LORD"; exhale, "'plans to give you hope and a future.'" (Repeat three times.) **Please open your eyes.**

Ask: **What did you feel as you thought on God's promise?** (Be prepared for a wide variety of answers.)

Activity

(Pass out Resource 5.) **In the Jewish tradition eulogizers are encouraged to do *hesped*—to create a balanced, accurate eulogy. The deceased had not just positive but also negative characteristics. The acrostic offers a way to identify all the characteristics that make up the unique person they grieve. You start by identifying one characteristic, positive or negative, that begins with each letter. *L* might be "loved" or "late"; *R* might be a "reader" or "religious."** (Give them permission to acknowledge negatives.)

So now reflect on your loved one and begin listing characteristics as rapidly as possible. Admittedly, some of the letters

may be difficult, such as Q and *Z*, but do the best you can. (You might pass out the sheets the week before you plan to use them so that individuals can have a week to create the eulogy. In sharing, depending on the number of persons in the group and time limitations, you might ask them to read their list, or to take a letter, say *A*, and go around, so that all the group members read aloud their *A*'s. Or you might ask participants to share the six most important characteristics they identified.)

Acrostics as Eulogies

Acrostics have long been a way that individuals wrote eulogies. If you had to describe your loved one's characteristics—positive and negative—using the ABC's, what would you include? Be honest! In the Jewish tradition *hesped* is a balanced eulogy that acknowledges the good as well as the bad. A false eulogy impedes reconciliation with the loss.

A ______________________	N ______________________
B ______________________	O ______________________
C ______________________	P ______________________
D ______________________	Q ______________________
E ______________________	R ______________________
F ______________________	S ______________________
G ______________________	T ______________________
H ______________________	U ______________________
I ______________________	V ______________________
J ______________________	W ______________________
K ______________________	X ______________________
L ______________________	Y ______________________
M ______________________	Z ______________________

It is difficult to believe that our weeks for this mutual-help group have gone by so quickly. Before we experience our final closing activity, I would like us to think about what has taken place in this group. First of all, let's take some time to look at our updated collages. Who would like to go first and show us what you have added in the blank half of the collage?

Words of hope

(Pass out Quote 7.)

"You may have heard
indeed you may believe
that your grief's journey end will come
when you resolve, or recover from,
your grief.

"But you may also be coming to understand
one of the fundamental truths of grief:
Your journey will never end.

"People do not 'get over' grief.
My personal and professional experience
tells me that a total return to "normalcy"
after the death of someone loved
is not possible;
we are forever changed
by the experience of grief."

—Alan D. Wolfelt, *The Journey Through Grief,* 135

Song

Each week we have listened to/sung a song. Many of our great hymns and gospel songs were written by grieving persons. Listen to this hymn. (Play CD; pass out Hymn Text 7.) (This may be eliminated if time becomes a factor in this session.)

He Giveth More Grace

(1)

He giveth more grace when the burdens grow greater;
He sendeth more strength when the labors increase.
To added affliction He addeth His mercy.
To multiplied trials, His multiplied peace.

(Refrain)

His love has no limit; His grace has no measure.
His pow'r has no boundary known unto men.
For out of His infinite riches in Jesus,
He giveth, and giveth, and giveth again!

(2)

When we have exhausted our store of endurance,
When our strength has failed ere the day is half done,
When we reach the end of our hoarded resources,
Our Father's full giving is only begun.

—Annie Johnson Flint* (*Sing to the Lord,* 101)

Note

If this is the last session, at this point, give each one a chance to comment on "what I have learned in this mutual-help grief group."

When all participants have had a chance to comment, proceed to "the naming" (chapter 4).

*"He Giveth More Grace," words by Annie Johnson Flint and music by Hubert Mitchell. © 1941, renewed 1969 Lillenas Publishing Company, Kansas City, MO 64141. Used by permission.

Remarks for Sharing at Final Session

(The facilitator may use these remarks as a closing summation for the group. Facilitators may edit, delete, or add their own thoughts.)

Grief can be a demanding taskmaster. In some ways, scaling Mount Everest might take less courage, be less demanding an adventure. By participating in this mutual-help grief group, you chose to grow. By coming back session after session, you chose to grow.

Remember those inch marks you placed on the doorjamb to record your height at different points in your childhood? Think back about your apprehensions about joining this group. Think about the first meeting. Do you see any signs of growth in yourself or in other members of the group? I do. You have hung out with some brave, remarkable people. You have accompanied one another through a section of the unknown territory called grief.

Now what?

Many of the lessons you have learned in these past weeks will prove valuable in the days and months ahead. Admittedly, because you have invested so much time in this support group, some will now expect you to be "over it." Some will expect you to be "all better" or "more like yourself." Yet the reality, as Melissa Gabbert and others have discovered, is that "no one ever talks about . . . how the hurt never really goes away. It's more like the ebb and flow of a tide, gradually moving you closer and closer to the shore of your soul"[1] or closer to the shore called reconciliation with the loss. The hurt does not go away—*it changes.*

You may still be wondering, "When will this, my grief, be over?" J. William Worden answers, "Asking when mourning is finished is a little like asking how high is up?" From his extensive experience as a grief therapist, he adds, "One benchmark of a completed grief reaction is when the person is able to think

of the deceased without pain. There is always a sense of sadness when you think of someone that you have loved and lost, but it is a different kind of sadness—it lacks the wrenching quality it previously had."[2] Your grief, hopefully, is no longer paralyzing. Hopefully, as a result of participating in this support group, you are more confident in saying, "My grief for [Name] counts."

Grievers understand these words of Mamie Eisenhower, a grieving mother, written in 1921: "I get so full up I have to tell someone, and I know you all share my feelings—and understand."[3] All grievers have "full up" moments. And one of the great places to share a "full up" moment for you has been a mutual-help grief group.

Your loved one is not "gone" or dead until two things happen: you stop saying the name, and you stop telling the stories about this loved one. Keep giving yourself permission to say the name and tell the stories. And keep giving yourself permission to grapple with your "if onlys."

I have come to appreciate the wisdom of Anne Brener's assessment that the goal of "successful" grief is to attempt "to transform our relationship with someone who has died from a wound to a blessing."[4] By participating in this grief group, you have done important grief work that will, in time, allow this wound to become a blessing. A blessing? Yes, a blessing.

> "A blessing, then, is anything that enters into the center of our lives and expands our capacity to resemble God's love, compassion, and goodness. A blessing may not always be painless, but it will always bring spiritual growth."
>
> —Wilkie Au[5]

The epitaphs on tombstones and grave markers are fascinating. On the marker of Lee Atwater, once chairman of the Republican Party and counselor to presidents Reagan and Bush, are these words: "I do not choose to be a common man. It is my God-given right to be uncommon."

Grievers can make a decision: "I do not choose to be a common *griever.* It is my God-given right to be uncommon."

I cannot take away your grief. Indeed, I would not ever do that. But from my own griefs, I would urge you, "Be uncommon." Keep grappling with all the complexities, ironies, and paradoxes of this grief season. Dare to utter the ancient words that Jacob confessed to his adversary that dark night: "I will not let you go unless you bless me" (Gen. 32:26).

The One who walked alongside grievers on the road to Emmaus is the One who will walk with us too—all the way home.

NOTES

1. M. Gabbert, "Holidays Without Mom," *Kansas City Star,* 15 December 1999, sec. F, 3.

2. J. William Worden, *Grief Counseling and Grief Therapy: A Handbook for the Mental Health Practitioner*, 2d ed. (New York: Springer, 1991), 18.

3. Susan Eisenhower, *Mrs. Ike: Memories and Reflections on the Life of Mamie Eisenhower* (New York: Farrar, Straus and Giroux, 1996), 18.

4. Anne Brener, *Mourning and Mitzvah: A Guided Journal for Walking the Mourner's Path Through Grief to Healing* (Woodstock, Vt.: Jewish Lights, 1993), 135.

5. Wilkie Au, *The Enduring Heart: Spirituality for the Long Haul* (New York: Paulist Press, 2000), 10.

RECOMMENDED READING

Books for pastors and facilitators

Albom, Mitch. ***Tuesdays with Morrie.*** **New York: Doubleday, 1997.**

Rarely has a book on death been a best-seller with seemingly a permanent niche on *the New York Times* best-seller list. But there was never quite a person like Morris Schwartz. Through the eyes of his student and friend, Mitch Albom, we learn a great deal about the last months of a dying friend's life.

Attig, Thomas. ***The Heart of Grief: Death and the Search for Lasting Love.*** **New York: Oxford University Press, 2000.**

One of the great grief issues is, "Now what?" Attig argues that rather than having to stop loving our deceased, we must learn to love them in new ways. Attig explores ways in which memories of loved ones can be sustained and valued.

Bernardin, Joseph Cardinal. ***The Gift of Peace.*** **Chicago: Loyola Press, 1997.**

In the final two months of his life, Cardinal Bernardin of Chicago shared his experience of "losing" the battle with cancer but gaining clarity and insight into the "gift" of a peaceful death. This is a spiritual classic.

Corr, Charles A., Clyde M. Nabe, and Donna M. Corr. ***Death and Dying: Life and Living.*** **2d ed. Pacific Grove, Calif.: Brooks/Cole Publishing, 1997.**

This is an *A-to-Z* compendium on dying, death, and bereavement. If you have a question about death, you may find, at least, part of the answer here.

Doka, Kenneth J., ed. ***Living with Grief: Children, Adolescents, and Loss.*** **Philadelphia: Brunner/Mazel, 2000.**

This is an incredible collection of practical short essays by some of the leading grief educators and therapists. This will give you valuable usable material on children and adolescents.

Fitzgerald, Helen. ***The Grieving Child: A Parent's Guide.*** **New York: Fireside/Simon and Schuster, 1992.**

"How will this death affect the children?" Explaining death and grief to children are challenging tasks. Fitzgerald offers practical, compassionate "been there" advice to help children cope with significant loss.

———. ***The Mourning Handbook.*** **New York: Simon and Schuster, 1994.**

Fitzgerald offers readers practical advice on what to expect and how to cope in this guidebook for the journey through grief.

Gamino, Louis A., and Ann Taylor Cooney. *When Your Baby Dies Through Miscarriage or Stillbirth.* Minneapolis: Augsburg, 2002.

The experience of miscarriage or stillbirth is a spiritually demanding experience. This resource, written by a grieving father, offers practical advice for parents and other family members. A book you will want to put in the grievers' hands.

Gilbert, Richard. *Finding Your Way After Your Parent Dies.* Notre Dame, Ind.: Ave Maria Press, 1999.

The death of a parent can be one of life's significant endings, particularly for adults. This book offers wise guidance for those who have lost one or both parents.

Grollman, Earl A., and Max Malikow. *Living When a Young Friend Commits Suicide or Even Starts Talking About It.* Boston: Beacon Press, 1999.

Thousands of teenagers attempt or commit suicide each year. Friends ask, "Why?" and "What more could I have done?" For every teen that commits suicide, dozens attempt it. This book offers practical advice on dealing with an individual who is talking about committing suicide. It offers wise insight for teenagers to "come to terms" with this loss.

Guest, A. G., comp. *A Little Book of Comfort: An Anthology of Grief and Love.* Grand Rapids: Marshall Pickering/Harper Collins, 1993.

Sooner or later grief's shadow touches all of us. This book is a compilation of "soul soothing" quotations that will be useful to the service planner as well as the griever.

Harris, Jill Werman, ed. *Remembrances and Celebrations: A Book of Eulogies, Elegies, Letters, and Epitaphs.* New York: Pantheon Books, 1999.

You've been asked to do a eulogy at a funeral. This book offers a wide range of resources from the funeral services of the famous and not so famous.

Huntley, Theresa. *When Your Child Dies.* Minneapolis: Augsburg, 2002.

The death of a child is the worst loss a parent can experience. This book by a skilled caregiver is a book you will want to keep on hand to share with parents.

———. *When Your Child Loses a Loved One.* Minneapolis: Augsburg, 2002.

Talking about a death with a child is a challenge—necessary but demanding. Huntley offers sage guidance in assisting a child in grief.

Lewis, C. S. *A Grief Observed.* New York: Bantam, 1961.

C. S. Lewis became something of an expert on grief during World War II. Then after four years of marriage to Joy Davidson, he was made a widower griever by her death. In 80 pages Lewis gives permission to people to do their grief work. This book has comforted millions of people. It is a must-read classic.

Magida, Arthur J., ed. *How to Be a Perfect Stranger: A Guide to Etiquette in Other People's Religious Ceremonies.* Vol. 1. Woodstock, Vt.: Jewish Lights Publishing, 1996.

In today's multicultural society, sooner or later you will have a friend who does not practice your faith (or any faith). How can you enter what the author calls "unfamiliar territory" without offense? This practical handbook offers advice not only on funerals but also on weddings, births, and special faith practices. This volume includes information on Buddhism, Hinduism, Islam, Judaism, selected Christian denominations, and Mormonism.

———, ed. *How to Be a Perfect Stranger: A Guide to Etiquette in Other People's Religious Ceremonies.* Vol. 2. Woodstock, Vt.: Jewish Lights Publishing, 1997.

This second volume offers insights into religious practices of smaller Christian denominations, as well as Baha'i and Sikh faiths. The reader gains insight into attending such events as weddings, funerals, and committals.

Manning, Doug. *Don't Take My Grief Away.* San Francisco: Harper and Row, 1979.

The title says it all—don't let anyone take away, limit, diminish, or disenfranchise your grief. This is a classic and a must for the counselor's shelf.

———. *The Funeral: A Chance to Touch, a Chance to Serve, a Chance to Heal.* Oklahoma City: In-Sight Books, 2001.

Grieving is not an enemy to be avoided; it is a process that leads to healing. One of the resources for healing is the funeral. Lots of people dislike funerals. But perhaps that is because they have not been to a good, well-prepared funeral. Manning powerfully addresses the question, "Why have a funeral?"

Martin, Terry L., and Kenneth J. Doka. *Men Don't Cry . . . Women Do: Transcending Gender Stereotypes of Grief.* Philadelphia: Brunner-Routledge, 1999.

Do men and women grieve differently? Nowhere are gender issues more pronounced than in grief and bereavement. There are lots of healthy ways for men and for women to do grief work. Lots of stereotypes about grief roles are challenged in this critical book.

McIntee, Jeanne Daly. *To Comfort, to Honor: A Guide to Personalizing Rituals for the Passing of a Loved One.* Minneapolis: Augsburg, 1998.

Funerals and memorial services are increasingly opportunities for personalization, to make them "reflect" the lives of the deceased. The ideas and examples offer possible ways to design a ritual to honor a loved one that does not seem like a "been to one/been to 'em all" experience. The reader will learn how to personalize a service.

Moe, Thomas. *Pastoral Care and Pregnancy Loss: A Ministry Long Needed.* Binghamton, N.Y.: Haworth Press, 1997.

This is a groundbreaking book offering guidance for ministry with those suffering pregnancy loss. The death of a baby can be a profound event for a couple, siblings, grandparents, and a congregation. This sensitive book will prepare you for significant ministry at the time of a most delicate loss.

Rupp, Joyce. *Praying Our Good-byes.* Notre Dame, Ind.: Ave Maria Press, 1988.

"Who can pray at a time like this?" grievers often ask. Yet the song urges, "Take it to the Lord in prayer." The author argues that instead of running from our losses, we should reflect on them, engage them, and pray them. The facts do not change, but we change through prayer.

Searle, Edward. *In Memoriam: A Guide to Modern Funeral and Memorial Services.* Boston: Skinner House, 1993.

If you are facing the loss of someone you know or having to plan a service (funeral or memorial service), this comprehensive guide gives you lots of practical advice and ideas.

Silverman, Phyllis Rolfe. *Never Too Young to Know: Death in Children's Lives.* New York: Oxford University Press, 2000.

This is the "gold standard" resource on children and death, dying, and bereaving. Offers a wonderful blend of current theory and practice. This resource is a must for your shelf.

Sittser, Gerald L. *A Grace Disguised: How the Soul Grows Through Loss.* Grand Rapids: Zondervan Publishing House, 1995.

Many individuals experience simultaneous multiple loss. Sittser lost three generations (daughter, wife, and mother) in a tragic automobile accident. In his own injuries, he became a single parent who had to reconstruct life without three key females in his life. Circumstances, the author argues, are not important. Rather it is eternally important what we do with those circumstances!

Smith, Harold Ivan. ***A Decembered Grief: Living with Loss When Others Are Celebrating.*** **Kansas City: Beacon Hill Press of Kansas City, 2000.**

Grievers have to survive the triathlon of holidays: Thanksgiving, Christmas, and New Year's. This easy-read book offers simple, practical ideas that grievers have found helpful.

———. ***Friendgrief: An Absence Called Presence.*** **Amityville, N.Y.: Baywood, 2001.**

Friends die. For some, "friendgrief" is an intrusion; for others, it is a continual factor shaping their emotional landscape. For many, the shaping losses of life will be when friends die. This book has valuable information on prayer and rituals.

———. ***Grieving the Death of a Friend.*** **Minneapolis: Augsburg, 1996.**

"Friendgrief" is one of the disenfranchised deaths in this culture. More than 10 million people are annually impacted by friends' deaths. Over 200 friend grievers offer insights from their experiences of losing friends.

———. ***Journaling Your Decembered Grief: To Help You Through Your Loss.*** **Kansas City: Beacon Hill Press of Kansas City, 2001.**

This is a resource to put in the hands of grievers who face the daunting task of "surviving" the triathlon of holidays: Thanksgiving, Christmas, and New Year's. This is a companion book for *A Decembered Grief.* Pastors will find many valuable quotations in this important resource.

———. ***On Grieving the Death of a Father.*** **Minneapolis: Augsburg, 1993.**

Fathers die. At whatever point in our life, the death of a father is a profound experience—even for those who did not have good relationships. Some 40 persons, such as George Bush, Lee Iacocca, Beverly Sills, and Dwight Eisenhower, offer insights from their experiences of losing their fathers.

———. ***When You Don't Know What to Say: How to Help Your Grieving Friends.*** **Kansas City: Beacon Hill Press of Kansas City, 2002.**

You can never "fix" an individual's grief. But there are ways you can "be" with a griever. Sharing another's grief is not about "fixing it" but about showing up.

———. ***When Your People Are Grieving: Leading in Times of Loss.*** **Kansas City: Beacon Hill Press of Kansas City, 2001.**

Individuals look to their pastors during the most personal, private, and vulnerable times of their lives: death, dying, and bereaving. As care leaders, pastors can supply mercy to grievers during these trying times. Each chapter concludes with a spiritual formation segment and a story that "will preach."

Spencee, Lina. ***Legacy: A Step-by-Step Guide to Writing Personal History.*** **Athens, Ohio: Swallow Press, 1997.**

Getting good material for eulogies from family members requires good questions. This book will give you "door-opener" questions that will aid your funeral/memorial service preparations.

Staudacher, Carol. ***A Time to Grieve: Meditations for Healing After the Death of a Loved One.*** **San Francisco: Harper/San Francisco, 1994.**

Grievers often need to borrow thoughts from others to make sense of their own losses. This book offers hundreds of quotations and brief easily read meditations and observations. It is a griever's friend.

Weems, Ann. ***Psalms of Lament.*** **Louisville, Ky.: Westminster John Knox Press, 1995.**

Ann Weems's son died on his 21st birthday. In poetry patterned from selected psalms, she elegantly pours out her lament.

Wolfelt, Alan D. ***Creating Meaningful Funeral Rituals: A Guide for Caregivers.*** **Fort Collins, Colo.: Companion Press, 1994.**

One of the "gifts" a griever can give is to plan and organize a meaningful funeral, memorial service, or special event. This workbook starts with the why but also leads planners methodically through this challenging task.

———. ***Healing a Friend's Grieving Heart.*** **Fort Collins, Colo.: Companion Press, 2001.**

This book has 100 practical ideas for helping someone through loss.

———. ***Healing Your Grieving Heart.*** **Fort Collins, Colo.: Companion Press, 2001.**

Within this book are 100 practical ideas that offer compassionate advice and simple activities to help a griever through the loss.

Wolpe, David. ***Making Loss Matter: Creating Meaning in Difficult Times.*** **New York: Riverhead Books, 1999.**

Not only is this an insightful book, but also it will be a wonderful resource for preaching material. After we experience significant personal losses, Wolpe asks, "How can we use the inevitable losses as sources of strength rather than despair?"

Worden, J. William. ***Grief Counseling and Grief Therapy: A Handbook for the Mental Health Practitioner.*** **3d. ed. New York: Springer, 2001.**

This is *the* book for those who counsel grievers or who lead support groups. Containing helpful information on grief and family systems, complicated mourning, and pathological grief, this book is a classic.

York, Sarah. *Remembering Well: Rituals for Celebrating Life and Mourning Death.* San Francisco: Jossey-Bass, 2000.

In these days of "celebrations of the life of . . . ," many people want innovations. This will be a helpful resource for planning a funeral or memorial service for individuals who are alienated from religious traditions or their families.

Zonnebelt-Smeenge, Susan J., and Robert C. DeVries. *Getting to the Other Side of Grief: Overcoming the Loss of a Spouse.* Grand Rapids: Baker Books, 1998.

"Till death us do part" is a sobering vow. This is a wonderful resource written by a clinical psychologist (Susan) and a pastor-professor (Robert). Both authors lost their spouses at a relatively young age. Their mix of psychological insights, biblical observations, and male and female perspectives will be a valuable book to recommend.

Books for children

Barron. T. A. *Where Is Grandpa?* New York: Philomel Books, 2000.

"Where is grandpa?" That is the question that haunts a boy when his grandfather dies. As the boy begins remembering all the familiar places he shared with his grandfather, he gains new insights into death.

Cohn, J. *I Had a Friend Named Peter: Talking to Children About the Death of a Friend.* New York: Morrow, 1987.

Beth's friend Peter is killed by a car. But Beth is blessed to have helpful parents and teachers respond to her grief. An accompanying adult section will also give guidance.

DePaola, Tommy. *Nana Upstairs and Nana Downstairs.* New York: Putnam, 1973.

One day young Tommy learns that his beloved great-grandmother is dead, but he does not believe it until he sees her empty bed. Through watching a falling star, Tommy comes to learn that Nana is now "upstairs."

Evans, Richard Paul. *The Dance.* New York: Simon and Schuster, 1999.

Dancing marks the rites of passage through a daughter's life. Her father is always watching her performances. But after his death, will she be able to dance again? This book describes "continuing bonds" and will delight adult readers as well as children.

Fox, Mem. *Wilfred Gordon McDonald Partridge.* New York: Harcourt and Brace, 1994.

Wilfred Gordon McDonald Partridge lives next door to an "old people's home." There he learns that memories are things that make you laugh, things that make you cry, or things as "precious as gold." This will help children talk about their memories of a loved one.

Garland, Sherry. *I Never Knew Your Name.* New York: Tichnor and Fields, 1994.

A small boy is saddened and confused by a tragedy he witnesses. But even more frustrating is that he never got to know the neighbor boy who commits suicide.

Munsch, Robert. *Love You Forever.* Scarborough, Ont.: Firefly Books, 1986.

One of the classics in children's literature, beloved by adults as well as children, is about a mother, who in various stages of her life, promises, "I will love you forever; I will love you for always." Then her son, after her death, takes on her loving words.

Rylant, Cynthia. *Dog Heaven and Cat Heaven.* New York: Blue Sky Press, 1997.

Great illustrations and a creative story line create a resource for pet lovers of any age who are grieving an animal's death.

Shriver, Maria. *What's Heaven?* New York: Golden Books, 1999.

When a loved one dies, it is easy to tell a child, "They've gone to heaven." But sooner or later the child will start asking questions about heaven. These questions in the book were originally asked when the author's grandmother, Rose Kennedy, died. The book will help children feel closer to heaven.

Viorst, Judith. *The Tenth Good Thing About Barney.* New York: Atheneum, 1971.

A cat dies, and a little boy tries to think of 10 good things to say about Barney at the funeral. He can only come up with 9 until he has an argument with a friend about whether cats go to heaven. He then comes up with the 10th thing.

Weir, A. B. *Am I Still a Big Sister?* Newtown, Pa.: Fallen Leaf Press, 1992.

This book responds to a nagging question of many children. It follows the progression from the illness, death, and ritualization of a girl's baby sister to the eventual birth of a new brother.

Zolotow, C. *My Grandson Lew.* New York: Harper, 1974.

A six-year-old wonders why his grandfather has not visited in a long time. Everything changes when he learns his grandfather has died.